Variations on Teaching and Supervising Group Therapy

Variations on Teaching and Supervising Group Therapy

Karen Gail Lewis
Editor

The Haworth Press
New York • London

RC
488
.V37
1989

Variations on Teaching and Supervising Group Therapy has also been published as *Journal of Independent Social Work*, Volume 3, Number 4 1989.

The Haworth Press, Inc., 10 Alice Street, Binghamton, NY 13904-1580
EUROSPAN/Haworth, 3 Henrietta Street, London, WC2E 8LU England

Library of Congress Cataloging-in-Publication Data

Variations on teaching and supervising group therapy / Karen Gail Lewis, guest editor.
    p. cm.
    "Has also been published as Journal of independent social work, volume 3, number 4, 1989" — T.p. verso.
    Includes bibliographies references.
    ISBN 0-86656-921-9
    1. Group psychotherapy — Study and teaching. 2. Group psychotherapy — Study and teaching — Supervision. I. Lewis, Karen Gail.
    [DNLM: 1. Psychotherapy, Group — education. W1 JO703AM v. 3 no. 4 / WM 430 V299]
RC488.V37   1989
616.89'152'07 — dc20
DNLM/DLC
for Library of Congress   89-19970
                                            CIP

Variations on Teaching and Supervising Group Therapy

CONTENTS

ABOUT THE EDITOR

Karen Gail Lewis, EdD, ACSW, is Associate Professor of Family and Group Therapy at the Catholic University of America, School of Social Services, Washington, DC. She is also Adjunct Professor, Department of Family and Child Development, Virginia Polytechnic Institute in Falls Church, VA.

Dr. Lewis has been practicing group therapy for about 20 years. She has taught group therapy to mental health professionals in graduate schools, community mental health agencies, hospitals, and public and private schools. She has also supervised therapy groups for children, adults, and couples, as well as groups of families. Dr. Lewis has experience leading specialized groups such as patients with cancer, couples with sexual difficulties, and children with behavior problems, as well as counseling general groups on such issues as lack of self-esteem and isolation.

Dr. Lewis has a master's degree in social work and a doctorate in counseling psychology and school consultation. She is certified as a clinician and supervisor of marriage and family therapy and as a group therapist. She is Co-Editor of *Siblings in Therapy: Clinical Issues and Life Span,* and is working on a co-authored book on multifamily groups and one on women's friendships. Dr. Lewis has published numerous articles and book chapters on group therapy (and family therapy), has presented papers both nationally and internationally, is on the editorial board of several professional journals, and is Book Review Editor for the *Journal of Independent Social Work.*

Introduction

> . . . Not one of all those who show an interest in my therapy and pass definite judgement upon it has ever asked me how I actually go about it. There can be but one reason for this, namely, that they think there is nothing to enquire about, that the thing is perfectly obvious.
>
> *Sigmund Freud, quoted in Schulman, 1979*
> *Foreword by William Schwartz, p. vii*

I suspect that most people supervising and teaching group therapy[1] learned by just doing it. I had taken a course in graduate school, and in my first job, I decided to run groups in order to elude an abusive supervisor who knew nothing about groups. Several years later I was asked to supervise the staff in a community mental health center who were being required to run groups. They knew little about group therapy; I knew little about supervising groups. The assumption that if you can do it you can teach it—as everyone knows—is not true! I suspect my experience is not very different than most group supervisors.

Scenario: A social worker takes two group work courses in graduate school and then joins the staff of a community agency. She is given permission by the administrator to run a group for low income single parents. However, she soon learns that verbal permission does not guarantee funds for equipment, a regularly available room, or time for preparation. Other problems she encounters include drop outs, lack of referrals from other clinicians, and monopolizing group members. She has supervision on her group and when it is over, she never runs another one.

1

It is very common, in my experience, to see a highly motivated social worker run one group and never try it again. Watching your eight member group slowly deplete to five, then four, then two is painful, demoralizing, and humiliating. Too many of these energetic social workers eventually stop running groups; they either lose faith in the power of groups or they blame themselves for being an inadequate therapist. However, a group supervisor can make a difference. Yet the schools of social work do not teach group supervision and there are few workshops on the topic.

For group therapists who want to start supervising but do not have the specialized training, the literature can be of some help if they want to run psychoanalytic groups. However, for those interested in one of the many other theoretical orientations or models, there is less help available. Many of the other orientations do not even mention teaching or supervising. Since people are running groups, I am left to wonder who taught them and how did their teachers learn.

This collection, then, is an attempt to fill this void for the different theoretical orientations of group therapy. *Variations on Teaching and Supervising Group Therapy* offers assistance to social workers who run groups but who lack the specialized training for becoming a supervisor.

The contributors were chosen to represent a cross section of the teachers of the various types of groups currently being run in America. Some are social workers and some come from other disciplines. This seems to represent the reality of what is happening as social workers learn about groups in the field. I have asked each of them to show what they do. The teaching audiences of the authors include experienced group therapists, professionals with little or no group therapy experience, and social work students. The teaching formats include one day workshops, semester long courses, year long training programs, once a week supervision, and outside consultation. The theoretical orientations include psychodynamic, family systems, psychodrama, gestalt, transactional analysis. The group work settings include family service agencies, child guidance centers, short-term health maintenance organizations, freestanding group training institutes, and private practice. The learning situations range from classroom to workshop, to training program, to agency supervision group.

The intent of this book is that you the reader will cull some ideas about supervising groups or about different theories or techniques to include in your current supervisory practice. The articles here may also provide some ideas as well as encouragement for an experienced group worker to begin providing supervision.

SUPERVISION OF GROUPS

Supervision of groups must attend to multiple levels of interaction. The role of the group supervisor is complex; she must attend to the multiple levels of interaction. The administrative and systemic issues of the group must be watched as well as the issues for the individual group members and for the group as a whole. Different modalities may place more emphasis on one or another of these factors, but they all are important in the smooth functioning of a group. Middleman and Rhodes (1985), authors of the only book solely devoted to supervision of social group work, list nine functions for the supervisor: humanizing, managing tension, catalyzing, teaching, helping with career socialization, evaluating, administering the workload, advocating for the supervisee, and assisting with procedural and programmatic changes. They also have a wonderful set of appendices of checklists and guidelines for new supervisors.

Coché (1978), a clinical psychologist, has a useful list of goals for training of group therapists. Supervisees need to learn the theoretical concepts — the book knowledge — and the skills for handling crises and repetitive patterns of problematic behaviors. They need to understand group dynamics and the interactions between two people's psychopathologies. They need to learn about transference phenomena and countertransference and how to use oneself in the therapy group.

Methods for the group supervision include verbal reporting on what happens in a group, direct observation of the group (in the room or through a one-way mirror), use of audio or videotapes, co-therapy with the supervisor. A frequent supervisory suggestion, and sometimes a requirement, is participation in a group for group therapy trainees.

Group therapy training is often provided in the model that is being taught. Theory and techniques used in the training will most likely reflect the modality of the leader of that group. For instance, a process training group in a school of social work will more than likely follow the beliefs of social work with groups; a training group for Transactional Analysis therapists will follow a TA model.

OVERVIEW OF THIS ISSUE

This becomes apparent in reading the articles in this volume, for all of the authors associated with a specific model use that format in their training. Each of the training models falls midway along the educational-therapeutic continuum, with some being more towards one than the other.

In the first article, Pfeffer, Epstein and Herrera look at the most commonly used format in group therapy today — psychodynamics. This is a joint paper written by the supervisor and two of the supervisees. They worked in a family service agency, met in a small group, and used their own process to understand the difficulties within their groups. Transference and countertransference are important factors in the supervision.

The second article is by Nicholas who uses family systems theory to understand the three subgroups that make up a group therapy supervision: the group, the co-therapists, and the supervisor/co-therapists. The examples used include graduate students and experienced therapists in individual supervision. She describes how energy is transmitted and utilized through the three subsystems.

The next four articles are on teaching Psychodrama, Gestalt, and Transactional Analysis to practicing therapists, and social work to students. Goldberg takes her readers through her one day Psychodrama workshop, demonstrating some of her exercises as well as explaining key concepts and the history of psychodrama. Napoli and Walk describe a nine-month Gestalt training program for practicing therapists who want to learn this treatment modality. The key concepts are described as well as the three aspects to the training program: personal growth, theoretical knowledge, and practical experience. Goulding describes a weekend Transactional Analysis training program, focusing on redecision therapy. His trainees are all practicing therapists who learn TA through their own growth experience. Ephross clarifies the confusion between social group work and group therapy. He describes some basic underpinnings of group therapy, creation of group exercises, and common fears about leading groups.

The next two articles address specific types of groups: children's groups and short-term groups. Coché describes the skills for a children's group therapy consultant. She also addresses student evaluations, the necessary knowledge base, and the required fit between the consultant and the institutional setting.

As insurance companies become more restrictive on the amount of mental health coverage they allow, short-term groups are becoming more prevalent. Daley and Koppenaal describe their experience in one of the oldest Health Maintenance Organizations (HMO) in this country. They present a model for a training program for therapists working in HMOs who are new to running short-term groups.

The final article, by Lewis, is on a theme that should be of vital interest to all who run groups — gender issues in the co-therapy team, in the supervision, and in the group itself. The supervisor's role in recognizing and addressing gender issues in all three levels is presented.

Variations on Teaching and Supervising Group Therapy should provide something for everyone. The hungry reader should be able to come away filled with new ideas, new concepts, new techniques, and hopefully, new energy for providing more training for a very viable mode of social work practice.

Karen Gail Lewis, ACSW, EdD

NOTE

1. The terms social work with groups, group therapy, group psychotherapy — while technically having different meanings — are used interchangeably in this text. Within schools of social work and among members of Association for the Advancement of Social Work with Groups (AASWG), the terms are clearly delineated. However, outside of this small but growing number of professionals, the distinctions are not clear. While there has been no study on how social workers learn to run groups, from my experience and my communication with others, it seems apparent that most social workers learn to run groups from whomever is

currently running them in their agency/organization. That may be a social worker, a psychologist, a psychiatric nurse, a psychiatrist, etc. The distinctions, so clear in theory, become blurred in the eclectic field of mental health.

For those interested in learning specifically about social work with groups are referred to: AASWG, c/o John Ramey, Membership Chair, Department of Social Work, University of Akron, Akron, OH 44325.

REFERENCES

Coché, E. (1978). Training of group therapists. In F. Kaslow & Associates (Eds.), *Supervision, consultation, and staff training in the helping professions*. San Francisco: Jossey-Bass, pp. 235-253.

Middleman, R. & Rhodes (1985). *Competent supervision: Making imaginative judgments*. Englewood Cliffs, NJ: Prentice Hall.

Chapter 1

Group Supervision: A Psychodynamic Perspective

Doris Pfeffer
Cynthia Epstein
Isabel Herrera

INTRODUCTION

This paper is jointly authored by the supervisor and two of the three supervisees who comprised a three-year supervision group for group therapists. The third participant has since left our geographical area and therefore was not a party to writing this article, nevertheless remaining an integral part of its contents.

Why a paper jointly authored? In our psychodynamic approach to group therapy mirrored in the supervisory group, we feel it important to give direct voice to the carriers of both cognitive and emotional learning; to transference and countertransference not only between therapists and their group members but also between members of the supervisory team. Since the supervisor — albeit in a different role — also is a participant in interactional learning, she will be considered a member of the group. In the interest of main-

Doris Pfeffer, MSW, is in private practice and is Consultant to Jewish Board of Family and Children's Services. She is also a part-time faculty member of the Smith College School of Social Work. Inquiries may be addressed to 295 Central Park West, #64, New York, NY 10024.

Cynthia Epstein, MSW, is in private practice and is affiliated with the Jewish Board of Family and Children's Services.

Isabel Herrera, MSW, is in private practice and is Group Therapy Consultant at the Jewish Board of Family and Children's Services.

taining the distinction, however, Doris Pfeffer will be referred to as the supervisor or in the first person when referring to herself.

In order to give individual and cooperative expression rather than amalgamation to different voices, this paper is both a joint and an individual effort organized in the following manner: Initial Description, Supervisory Method, and Theoretical Formulations are written by Doris Pfeffer; The Process of Learning is written by Isabel Herrera and Cynthia Epstein; Supervisor's Affective and Transferential Experience and Concluding Statement are written by Doris Pfeffer; the Postscript is written by Isabel Herrera and Cynthia Epstein.

INITIAL DESCRIPTION

Doris Pfeffer was a social work supervisor and Assistant Director of Group Therapy for the counseling division of the Jewish Board of Family and Children's Services in New York City at the time this group was formed. The supervisees were social workers with a range of experience in individual psychotherapy from two to five years, having each led a therapy group for one year at the time they joined our supervision group. They were each supervised individually during the initial year by the supervisor.

Doris Pfeffer is a single, middle-aged woman, approximately ten years older than Judy, the eldest of the three other participants. Her family of origin consisted of a younger sister, herself, and their parents. Judy, in her mid-forties when the group formed, had been divorced, remarried, and was the mother of two grown sons. She came from a family of five children, she being the youngest, the adored child, and only girl. Judy's appearance will be described because it played a role in emerging transferences to be discussed subsequently. She is a striking-looking woman with a head of curly auburn hair; she is highly emotionally expressive, and flamboyant in style. Cynthia, in her early forties, was divorced, with two teenage daughters, and remarried. She comes from a family where she was the elder of two girls and, like the supervisor, felt like the parentified child. She is a deeply introspective, sometimes humorously sarcastic woman of decided intellectual bent. Isabel, in her early thirties, had been at the agency the longest of the three — five years. She had, however, less experience both as a group therapist and working with the supervisor when she joined the group a year after its formation. She is a single woman, born in Cuba, but having spent most of her life in the United States. She is the younger of two children, with an older brother. Isabel was the only non-Jewish member of the group in a Jewish agency, where the client population is racially, religiously, and ethnically diverse. She is an outspoken young woman who gives easy expression to her enthusiasms, criticisms, and particularly to her desire to experiment and to use approaches in her work that did not necessarily conform to the "supervisor's approach."

The group was formed because the agency and the supervisor believed that the group training method, mirroring to the extent that it does group therapy, is the most efficacious manner in which to supervise group therapists. Since, however, it required more training time, it was not widely used. The supervisor in this situation decided to ask Judy and Cynthia if they would like to be supervised together. They both were leading open-ended therapy groups, which were not time-limited or symptom-focused, and interested in deepening their knowledge of the group psychodynamic approach. They were considered by the supervisor to be on the same general level regarding knowledge of group therapy; both showed strong potential for further development. To the supervisor they seemed talented and motivated and had had a positive experience in their individual supervision with her. This seemed important because this change necessitated that everyone who participated give some of her own time. The agency's productivity requirements limited the extra supervision time credit available. The group's initial experience as a positive, rich, learning endeavor fairly readily became known in the office. The laughter, the sense that we were a "group," having fun, is important because it implied to us that we were somehow "special."

One member of the staff was consulted by the supervisor as to whether or not she would like to join the group — if it were possible to extend the time — because she was the most experienced group therapist in the office (several years more than the present group members, although not necessarily more knowledgeable). It should not be overlooked that this young woman and the supervisor were having some difficulties in their relationship as supervisor and supervisee. She was interested in joining the group but not "available." Another staff member wanted to join but she was told that in this particular group we were dealing with less goal-directed groups than the one she was leading (a group for women seeking to change careers). This applicant had considerable prior experience in career counseling which strongly influenced her work as both individual and group therapist.

When Isabel requested group membership, however, the supervisor readily submitted her application to Judy and to Cynthia. The group had been meeting for one year at this juncture. Isabel's interest was greeted positively even though it required that each of the present members contribute an additional fifteen minutes of her own time. We now had a supervisor and three supervisees, a greater variety of groups and therapists. Isabel's group consisted of young men and women manifesting relationship and career problems; Judy's, of middle-aged men and women dealing with life transitions; and Cynthia's, of single mothers coping with a wide variety of issues.

It became clear at this point to the supervisor and to the supervisees that there was a selective process, going on in the supervisory group that had to do with something other than a prospective new member's experience, interest, or competence. This seemed related to the relationship of said member to the supervisor, to her "interest" in them, to transference and countertransference.

The group met in the supervisor's office. We sat in a circle, although the supervisor placed her chair next to the desk — thus situating herself alongside the prop of centrality. Everyone spontaneously took the same seats; Judy next to the supervisor, Cynthia on her other side but further distanced, Isabel next to Cynthia almost on the opposite side of the room from the supervisor (the traditionally regarded confrontational position). Judy invariably arrived early. It should be noted that her office was a few doors away while Cynthia's and Isabel's were on another floor.

SUPERVISORY METHOD

The supervisory method was similar to that used by psychodynamically oriented group therapists. The process of teaching was not that distinct. No one was ever called upon to present or told what to do unless she directly asked; more often than not the supervisor deflected questions from herself to the training group. The supervisor pointed out themes and consciously tried to direct the group toward examining issues of transference, countertransference, and resistance. The one method used by the supervisor which was not a replication of processes used in therapy groups was that of role-playing. At first the supervisor played the role of therapist, with the supervisees assuming roles of group members who had been described by the therapist of the group. Gradually other members of the training group played the therapist's role. It is important to point out that the purpose of this was not to show the group therapist whose group we were role-playing "how to do it," but rather to enable the emergence into conscious recognition of the transference and countertransference issues of which the group leader was not aware. This cast the group into an experiential mold which was probably responsible in significant measure for the character it quickly assumed — one where cognitive and emotional learning was taking place simultaneously and where parameters between training and therapy for the supervisory group needed to be constantly noted. This was done by allowing personal life material to emerge, but redirecting it back to the group being conducted by the trainee, and using its emotional force to gain greater insight into the therapy group's reaction to like material.

I recall that a member of one of the groups stimulated a discussion between Judy and Cynthia regarding their anger at their ex-husbands. I allowed this to continue until one of them said, "Okay, I've blown my stack. I can get back to presenting my group. What does it have to do with my group? Am I overidentifying with Molly or stimulating her anger in an unconscious or inappropriate way?" These possibilities were discussed and pondered. They needed to be considered as part of the transference-countertransference matrix.

THEORETICAL FORMULATIONS

Having described the setting, structure, process of formation, and general comments on supervisory method, we will now spell out what we mean when we refer to these groups as "psychodynamic." Perry, Cooper, and Michels (1987) present us with an excellent starting point in stating that

> One common misconception is that a psychodynamic formulation is indicated only for those patients in a long-term, expressive psychotherapy. This belief ignores the fact that the success of any treatment may involve supporting, managing, or even modifying aspects of a person's personality. The therapeutic effectiveness or failure often hinges on how well or poorly the therapist understands the patient's dynamics and predicts what resistances the patient will present and designs an approach that will circumvent, undermine, or surmount these obstacles. (p. 543)

By using a psychodynamic model we are drawing upon a theoretical construct that gives attention to psychoanalytic theory as it has expanded, developed, and shifted over time. We give cognizance to early preoedipal influences on development, to the importance of defensive systems as adaptive and/or protective of the ego, and to object relations theory in addressing internalized representations of self and other.

In group therapy particularly, where the patient's interpersonal world is dramatized before us on a simulated family stage, it behooves the therapist to be aware of the present replications of the past as manifested through characterological ways of being in the world in relation to the self, to others, and to the enactment of powerful transferences and resistances; here defenses operate to protect the ego against the onslaught of feelings induced by other group members as well as by the therapist. It is for this reason that countertransference reactions in the therapist must be given careful attention so as to preclude premature confrontation, which is anathema to the psychodynamically oriented group therapist.

Transference and countertransference necessarily complement one another. They form a functioning unity. Each conditions the other and consequently forms a transference-countertransference equation. Countertransference can come from distorted reactions, from sources in the therapist's past and present psychic state, or from reactions to the patient's transference. Just as countertransference is the psychological response to the patient's real and imagined (by the therapist) transference, so is transference the response to the therapist's real and imagined countertransference. What seems central in our view is to recognize that there are essentially two types of countertransference — one emanating from the therapist's inner world and the other a reaction to the patient's transference. That these are not neatly separated at all times goes without saying, but it is essential to differentiate between them since the subject state reaction of the therapist — variously referred to in the literature as subjective countertransference, countertransference proper, the therapist's transference — is an impediment to treatment when it remains unprocessed, imbedded in the therapist's unconscious. The countertransference reaction to the patient's transference, on the other hand — referred to as objective or induced countertransference — is an essential vehicle for understanding the patient. Some have gone so far as to regard it as the central agent in the therapist's dynamic use of self in the treatment process.

It is generally accepted that not all patients can be treated for characterological change exclusively in group therapy. But even in addressing ourselves to short-term groups with very circumscribed goals — such as the very common bereavement groups which often run about twelve sessions — we turn again to Perry, Cooper, and Michels (1987), who warn us that only the therapist who formulates the specific meaning of the patient's illness or oppressive psychological situation in terms of developmental issues can be prepared to communicate in a beneficial and ultimately empathic way. They state, for example, that

> a pseudo-humanitarian approach, a form of verbal hand-holding that does not consider the character style of a particular patient may be experienced by paranoid patients as intrusive, by histrionic patients as seductive, by obsessive patients as demeaning, by depressed patients as undeserving and guilt-provoking, and by dependent or phobic patients as sanction for further regression or avoidance. (p. 546)

As psychodynamically oriented group therapy clinicians, what we are saying most emphatically is that interventions are heard differently by different patients in the same context and by the same patient in different contexts. Consequently, both the individual (patient) and the context (group culture) must be understood by the therapist. While it may be both comfortably profitable and creative for the filmmaker to lend symbolic ambiguity to his work, we as therapists must be responsible for what we stimulate as we seek to understand and to heal.

To get back to context, we must deal with the concept of group. Are we treating the group, individuals in a group, or individuals through the group? Margaret Rioch (1970), discusses the work of Wilfred Bion, the innovator of the group-as-a-whole approach and his treatment of the group as the patient. Rioch informs us that to conclude from this that Bion believed in the existence of a group mind (as he has been accused in the literature) is erroneous. According to Rioch, the group mind is a distorted figment of the imagination and emerges when people are threatened with loss of their individual distinctiveness. That this occurred in a variety of non-therapy groups has been demonstrated, sometimes tragically, throughout history — within nations and in special interest groups — paraded under banners of morality, religion, and political ideologies. Freud (1921) wrote of this phenomenon, the demonic power of the mob, in his only paper on group psychology.

As group therapists we must therefore be attuned to group forces, to the basic unconscious assumptions that Rioch and Bion describe, assumptions from which groups operate, the latent operable themes.

Sy Ethan (1987) also addresses himself to this in maintaining that

> The group may be seen as a unified system of interacting individual minds and characters, each individual finding expression through characteristic languages, gestures, and postures. The group thus seen has both a unified nature of its own and a diversity of members in a sustained dynamic state. (p. 375)

This is very close to Henry Ezriel (1980), who stresses unconscious need systems, basing much of his work on Melanie Klein's concept of unconscious object relations. This led Ezriel to a discussion of interlacing transferences in groups, forming what he calls the central group tension dominating at any particular point in time. Some supervisors and authors call this the group focal point or theme.

Leonard Horwitz (1977) has distilled the contributions of Bion, the expansion and refinements of Ezriel and others into a workable model which places the group-as-a-whole concept within the framework of treating patients for individual goals in a group context. In other words, treating the individual through the group.

The subject of resistance is ultimately central in all treatment but particularly in group therapy because of the factor of contagion. When one member threatens to leave, everyone's desire to separate prematurely, to escape the fantasied prison, to protest against the group or the therapist's "invasion" may be stimulated. Rosenthal (1987) discusses this as defense mechanism. It is the therapist's responsibility to determine whether or not it is adaptive or maladaptive. This becomes important as we work to separate our understanding of the individual from the group and to examine the interplay between the need to belong and the need to separate.

THE PROCESS OF LEARNING

Entering the Supervisory Group

Cynthia: When I was asked to lead a long-term psychotherapy group composed of single mothers I felt both flattered and somewhat intimidated. There were a number of such women in my caseload I felt would benefit from a group experience. I was fond of them, empathized with their struggles, and was eager to offer them additional help. On the other hand, I felt that I might jeopardize a treatment that was going well since I was unfamiliar with the group modality. However, the promise of weekly individual supervision enabled me to overcome my reluctance.

In the course of the year, my supervision experience shifted from individual to conjoint to group. I had little resistance to these changes because each brought new learning opportunities, they were incremental and voluntary, and I liked my colleagues and trusted the supervisor's judgement.

Isabel: I became a member of this group after one year of individual supervision. From the beginning I felt permission to leave behind a self-imposed (and elsewhere rewarded) analytic restraint and dive headlong into the often-charged group dynamics. The supervisory group was partly experiential in nature, with highly expressive people whom I generally liked and respected. I come from a family where it was not safe to freely express one's emotions, particularly those confrontational ones. You had to be alike in order to belong. This group was different, not my fragile family. Indeed, I found that its members would not fall apart as I became more myself, although my sensitivity to this issue may have been more unconscious than conscious at the time I joined.

The Group Experience

In our supervision group we both experienced and observed the unfolding of the developmental stages of a group. To do this required that we freely shift back and forth among the levels of experience and perspectives evoked by the interaction. These included: (1) emotionally interacting and then analyzing both content and process; and (2) relating the learning in the training group to the groups we were leading.

It was a tribute to the supervisor's skill that the teaching/learning experience moved with a seamless flow, never feeling inauthentic or contrived. Perhaps we can convey what it was like to be a member of "our group" by presenting a series of vignettes which illustrate the stages of group development, the nature of the supervisor's interventions, and the members' responses at various significant points in the group's history.

Early Phase

Though Cynthia and Judy had been meeting with the supervisor for approximately one year prior to the addition of Isabel, it is from Isabel's arrival that the history of "our group" is reckoned.

> Cynthia, Judy, and the supervisor are sitting in their customary places when Isabel arrives, looks around nervously, and takes a vacant chair opposite the supervisor. A discussion of one of Judy's difficult clients ensues, and shortly thereafter the

supervisor notices that Isabel is writing something down. With annoyance, she questions Isabel about her writing, indicating that she considers this a violation of confidentiality. As an aside, the supervisor asks Isabel if she is planning to write an article. Isabel anxiously attempts to explain that she is merely jotting something down which she feels applies to her own group. Cynthia and Judy remain aloof while Isabel seems extremely uncomfortable.

As this interaction was explored in the following sessions, a number of phenomena typical of the early phase of group development were identified. There was little interaction among the members. Instead, all of the "elders" used Isabel's unfamiliarity with the already established norm of not writing about other people to highlight her outsider status and to reinforce their own positions. This interfered with Isabel's attempt to make a place for herself within the group and may have also served to deflect attention from the task of dealing with a difficult treatment issue or conflicts between old members and the supervisor. Thus individual and group needs and vulnerabilities found expression in the exclusion of Isabel. Also observed at this phase, though by no means restricted to it, was parallel process, exemplified by the parallelism between Isabel's difficulties in entering the supervision group and those she had encountered in her own group, where she replaced a well-loved therapist who had left the agency. This process is also illustrated by the following vignette:

Isabel complains that she is having a great deal of trouble with Joan, who continually expresses dissatisfaction with the group, mainly conveying that nothing it does is of any value to her. Isabel then recounts the numerous attempts and strategies she has employed, all to no avail. They are experienced by Joan not only as useless, but actually assaultive. Isabel, frustrated and furious, brings this problem to the supervisory group.

Cynthia, Judy, and the supervisor (whom we always called Doris) respond by offering a variety of "helpful" suggestions, all of which Isabel says she has already tried unsuccessfully, or which she is sure will be as ineffective as those she has already used.

Faced with this stalemate, in which Isabel was reenacting the role of Joan, the supervisor invited Isabel to join her in a role play.

> *Isabel (playing Joan)*: I really don't see why I should stay in this group. They always criticize me, no one here understands me, and after I go home I always feel worse. I thought therapy was supposed to make things better.

> *Supervisor (playing the Therapist)*: You are right. I am certainly not going to suggest that you continue to suffer in this group. But before you leave, it would be helpful for you to have an understanding of why it that you never feel you get any help.

This intervention enabled Isabel to enter Joan's world and experience what it was like to feel constantly misunderstood and attacked—beyond help. The terror of this position, which Isabel experienced in the supervision group as she became Joan, allowed her to move away from her anger and frustration and to explore her complex countertransference—induced and otherwise. By sharing their reactions, Cynthia and Judy enabled Isabel to understand what it was like for the members of her group to deal with Joan, although it was not until a later stage that the supervision group focused on the personal implications of this incident for Isabel.

As noted earlier, at the beginning stage of our group, initial maneuvers were directed toward separating the older members from the newest one. There was an emphasis on difference. This stage gave way rather quickly, however, to one in which we became strongly identified with each other as a group. There was an unconscious tendency for members to wear the same clothes, and jokes about selecting a group uniform were rampant. Significant amounts of food were brought to sessions, with the underlying feeling that this was a "well-catered affair." This feasting seemed to serve a variety of purposes: it set the supervision group apart from the groups we led, reduced anxiety, and fostered the feeling that ours was a kind and generous family. It also enhanced group identity and cohesion and tested the limits of the supervisor, who seemed both comfortable with and indulgent of the way in which we conducted ourselves and was thereby very much a part of the group, though still differentiated from it.

At this point we all seemed well fed and clothed and felt comfortable in revealing problems we were having with our own groups. However, this behavior was also a form of acting-out of unconscious rivalries and resistance to the work of the group, which was to find more direct expression in a later stage.

During the early phase, the supervisor's role was to facilitate the formation of the group and to present an attitude of benign interest in understanding the nature of the interactions among us. We brought group problems to supervision just as our group members would bring "real life" concerns to the therapy group. These would provoke an interactional process which would then be examined by all of us.

Middle Phase

This rather gala initial phase was followed by the emergence of conflict and rivalry. Each of us had apparently staked out a role in the group that was similar to that in our family of origin or had adopted behavior that, though ostensibly different, would push us back into our old positions. Thus Isabel, who had been unable to confront her parents, became generally obstreperous, giving voice to the group's unconscious aggression toward the supervisor/parent, which differentiated her from the other children. This role, however, did not lead to her expulsion from the group as it did from her family, but instead served to identify and secure her place within it. Judy, the only sister among four brothers, gravitated toward the familiar center stage of her childhood through her flamboyantly expressive behavior. Cynthia, the parentified child, regularly dished up the sober voice of reason and reconciliation which was occasionally interspersed with sardonic, humorous comments, lending intensity to her presence in the group. The supervisor thus provided the screen for parental projections.

Isabel complains that there are no men for her group—Judy has them all. She describes her various unsuccessful attempts to recruit new men and even when she finds one who is promising, he then decides to leave the city. She complains that the man she is dating should be in her group, not in her life.

Judy becomes a bit apologetic, saying that the men in her group are not so great, that they are old, and really it's not her fault that she has several men in her group and Isabel has only one.

Cynthia, Ms. Sobriety, suggests that Isabel is carrying on too much. What's the big deal about having men in the group? (Cynthia has an all-female group.)

The supervisor then volunteers to kill off all the men in Judy's group so that she won't have more than Isabel.

The supervisor's use of the outrageous or of carrying a thinly veiled yet unconscious wish to the extreme was a very powerful group intervention, which became known as "doing a Doris." It broke the tension and opened the way to a discussion of envy, sibling rivalry, and aggression. It was also apparent in this situation that significant personal material for Judy and Isabel had been activated by group issues, and was being presented as group problems. Since group members knew quite a lot about each other, the countertransference issues were noted and referenced back to the therapy groups. This vignette provides an example of the way in which the therapists' issues may be activated in the therapy group and then played out and examined in supervision.

The transferences and learning experiences were not confined to those between the therapists and the members of their groups. They also involved interactional problems among members of the supervisory team.

Cynthia is describing a difficulty she is having with a client in her group who has consistently yet quietly challenged her ability as a therapist. At present this client is thinking of leaving the group; she is extremely busy and is also in individual treatment, which she claims is more helpful.

The supervisor turns to Judy and asks for her opinion. Cynthia notices Isabel's irritation at this interchange, but does not comment. Cynthia then responds to Judy's observation by saying it doesn't feel quite right. The supervisor *again* turns to Judy for comment.

Isabel, who can no longer contain her frustration, points our that the supervisor has twice solicited Judy's opinion while completely ignoring her presence. She feels that the supervisor favors Judy. Cynthia supports Isabel's view. Judy then criticizes Cynthia for her generally sarcastic tone. The supervisor notes that Judy is protecting her from the anger of the other members.

This meeting was significant for many reasons. As the supervisor was away the following week, the group met without her and together agreed that we all felt that Doris favored Judy. Our meeting led to an exploration of roles played in our families of origin, which brought clarity to our behavior and reactions to one another. Much anger was relieved as the siblings united against the supervisor-maternal object, who was not told about the meeting. Cynthia understood her support of Isabel not only as a reality validation but more significantly as an unconscious identification with Isabel's ability to challenge the authority. Judy's expression of distress about her position as favored child in the group supervisory family reduced the envy toward her. The impact of these disclosures was later manifested in the group by a decrease in Judy's dramatic presentations and by Cynthia and Isabel competing more constructively and successfully for the supervisor's attention.

These shifts were reflected in more mature relationships, which included a de-idealization of the supervisor and the acceptance of a more egalitarian relationship with her. The opportunity for the emergence of multiple transferences was also demonstrated in this phase of the group.

In this middle stage the supervisor rigorously focused on the interactive flow of process and helped the group to tolerate and explore negative affects such as hostility, anger, jealousy, and envy, thereby facilitating the integration of the positive and negative aspects of interpersonal relationships. Transferences shifted, yielding to a better reality orientation and decreased dependence on the supervisor.

Termination Phase

The training group was faced with a premature termination. Within the space of two weeks, Judy announced her plans to leave the state and to terminate at the agency within six weeks, and the supervisor to drastically cut back her hours. In essence, this signaled the demise of "our group." The shock waves reverberated throughout our supervision and therapy groups.

Cynthia and Isabel, the abandoned ones, acted out in their own groups. Cynthia uncharacteristically revealed personal information. Isabel felt a growing resentment of her group's neediness as well as a desire to become one of its members. Supervision helped to clarify these behaviors as a reaction to the loss of our group and to the wish to demonstrate to the supervisor the dire consequences of her departure. As a group we coped with this termination by reverting to earlier forms of gratification, such as planning a lunch at a fancy French restaurant.

While the group may have continued productively had Judy and the supervisor stayed, the seeds for its end were being sown by the supervisees' growing professional competence. Whereas in the beginning we had introjected the supervisor to some extent, i.e., trying to "do a Doris," by wishing she would be in the therapy room with us, we had now been able to digest her, so that the introject became integrated, and our own styles more distinct.

SUPERVISOR'S AFFECTIVE
AND TRANSFERENTIAL EXPERIENCE

To the supervisor this was one of the most interesting experiences of her supervisory career. The characteristics of the group that made it a lively, dynamic learning experience have already been discussed so I will focus on the personal and transferential elements for me and what I consider to have been their impact upon my role as supervisor.

Judy, Cynthia, and Isabel represented different parts of myself—

in time and in an ongoing counterpoint in the continual transformations of the self. Judy in her expressive flamboyance, trying to harness herself to a more reflective anchor, reminded me of myself as a therapist and younger woman: the actor-outer who reached for containment. Cynthia represented that reflective, more intellectual self trying to understand and to mediate in my somewhat chaotic and what seemed to me overly expressive family. Isabel represented the rebelliousness of my youth, the reconstructed rebel of my adulthood which jealously I realized she in her early thirties still has permission to express and at times act upon, while I do not. So the group created a paradigm of a whole wished-for fantasy self for me and enabled identifications, transference reactions, and enjoyment in working with all of its members. While this can be enriching, it must be understood and not just experienced by the supervisor. Otherwise, it will be acted out or picked up by the supervisees, unprocessed, thereby creating through unconscious forces a counterproductive, unharnessed series of events.

Now to speak to a transference of a special order in that it pervaded the group with varying degrees of force throughout its life and remained an ultimately unresolved, although not an unworkable issue. Judy has previously been referred to by the other supervisees as my "favorite." To me initially she was the woman with the full set of auburn curls who arrived first and sat next to me. When she walked in, I was immediately and for some seconds thereafter aware of her hair, which I loved. When the others arrived, the group meeting began and my awareness of Judy's curls was no longer part of my consciousness. Then my mother died—suddenly and unexpectedly. After a week I returned to work and that day Judy arrived first as usual for our meeting. I blurted out, aware of the strong regressive feelings I had been having all week, "You have such beautiful hair; just like my mother's when I was a child—before she became old." By the time Cynthia and Isabel arrived, the incident was over but my consciousness of it and my special transference to Judy and what she symbolized for me remained. It was a transference that connected me not only to my mother but to myself as a young child. Was Judy then my "favorite" or did favorite mean that I moved her into the position of introjected object of mother at regressive moments for me in the life of the group?

What also seems important here is that Judy's experience as the favorite child in her family of origin was recapitulated for her and abetted by the other members of the group. One can only speculate what supervisor or supervisees would have done with that head of hair on another body, another psyche, a supervisee whose life experience had heretofore cast her differently.

I think this experience intensified feelings and enhanced learning. It taught us all that multiplicity of transferences and countertransference reactions when understood can be an enrichment to supervision. I find it interesting that there was a resistance on the part of the group to giving up the group supervisee as mother and accepting her as child. I had at one point discussed the nature of my transference to Judy with the group. They either forgot or dismissed this and continued — Judy included — to view her as preferred, while I struggled in transferential memory both to remain in and to extricate myself from this position.

CONCLUDING STATEMENT

The confluence of transferences can be jarring, reparative, or hauntingly reminiscent. It is essentially the resistance to their recognition, the supervisor's ability or inability to understand his/her own transference feelings toward the supervisee group and its individual members who are being presented, that facilitates or interferes with those factors — beyond understanding of theory and technique — which make for failure or success in treatment and supervision.

The question as to whether or not the supervisor (and to a lesser extent the supervisees) inadvertently chose members toward whom they had a positive transference has already been addressed. Quite clearly, this characterized and influenced what occurred and what was learned. This is not to ignore the periods of interactional tension in our group. But one could say that the cards were stacked in a particular transferential direction which may have contributed to learning in some areas and limited it in others. In a different group we may have laughed less, felt less "special," but we might also have had to come to stronger grips with possible negative forces that lay unrevealed in our feelings toward each other and among the supervisees toward those members of their therapy groups who aroused the most negative feelings.

As time went on, I, the supervisor, became less centrally located. The supervisees developed a peership of mutual enablement as a result of professional growth and development and growing trust among themselves.

The group supervision experience allows a multiplicity of relationships to emerge and to be examined in living community which is not only a mirror of group therapy but of how we live in the world.

POSTSCRIPT

We have been brought together again, albeit perhaps ironically without Judy, for the writing of this paper, which has provided the opportunity for reflection with some distance and tranquillity on the ways in which the group affected us both personally and professionally. Central to this increased understanding was the supervisor's recognition and sharing with us of the role played by her transference to Judy, the manifestations of which were experienced by group members as a special preference. In fact, it was this issue and the multiplicity of group and individual reactions to it that might be referred to in Ezriel's terms as the "focal group tension." Thus commitment to ongoing self-scrutiny in which the transferential reactions of the therapist/supervisor are as much an object of analysis as those of the client was powerfully conveyed to us through this experience and has become our central legacy.

REFERENCES

Ethan, Sy. (1987). "Some Connections between Individual and Group Therapy." *The Psychoanalytic Review*, Vol. 74, No. 3, pp. 373-385.

Ezriel, Henry. (1980). "A Psychoanalytic Approach to Group Treatment." Saul Scheidlinger, ed., *Psychoanalytic Group Dynamics*. International Universities Press.

Freud, Sigmund. (1921). "Group Psychology and the Analysis of the Ego." *The Collected Works of Sigmund Freud*.

Horwitz, Leonard. (1977). "A Group-Centered Approach to Group Psychotherapy." *International Journal of Group Psychotherapy*, Vol. 27, No. 4, pp. 423-439.

Perry, Samuel; Cooper, Arnold, and Michels, Robert. (1987). "The Psychodynamic Formulation: Its Purpose, Structure, and Clinical Application." *The American Journal of Psychiatry*, Vol. 144, pp. 543-550.

Rioch, Margaret. (1970). "The Work of Wilfred Bion in Groups." *Psychiatry*, Vol. 33, pp. 56-66.

Rosenthal, Leslie. (1987). *Resolving Resistance in Group Psychotherapy*. Jason Aronson.

Chapter 2

A Systemic Perspective of Group Therapy Supervision: Use of Energy in the Supervisor-Therapist-Group System

Mary W. Nicholas

Psychotherapy supervisors are rarely trained in supervision before they are promoted into that role (Alonso, 1985). Often such advancement conforms to "the Peter Principle," the notion that people in organizations rise to their own level of incompetence. Group therapy is very difficult to do, let alone supervise; and yet, training opportunities in group therapy are rare compared to what is available for the individual or family therapy practitioner. Practically no courses exist on the supervision of group therapy, and in many mental health settings, what passes for supervision of therapy groups is just a review of individual cases in the group.

Given the enormous complexity of the task of psychodynamic group therapy supervision, I have found it useful, if not essential, to think of it systemically. I will explain briefly why I believe a systemic perspective is important for group therapy supervision. Using case examples from my own supervision of group therapy, I will describe how energy is transmitted and utilized throughout the entire "therapy group system," by which I mean the group, the therapists, and the supervisor. While I will only elaborate on this one

Mary W. Nicholas, MSW, MEd, PhD (cand.), is in private practice and is Clinical Instructor at the Department of Psychiatry, Yale School of Medicine. Inquiries may be addressed to 103 Eeckett Avenue, Branford, CT 06405.

27

application of systems theory to the group therapy supervision process, this discussion could be extended at another time to include other aspects of systemic thinking in relation to group therapy supervision.

BACKGROUND FOR A SYSTEMIC APPROACH
TO GROUP THERAPY SUPERVISION

I acquired my familiarity with systems thinking through my study of the hypnotic and strategic techniques of Milton Erickson (Haley, 1963, 1973; Lankton & Lankton, 1983). The notion of circularity, the idea that change occurs naturally through disorder and reorganization at a higher level (Watzlawick, 1974), the use of paradox to force new paradigms and frames of reference (Haley, 1963), and the systemic analysis of verbal and nonverbal levels of communication (Watzlawick, 1967) — all of these are potentially applicable not only to group therapy (Nicholas, 1984), but to the supervision of group therapy as well.

My motivation for developing a systems view of group therapy supervision is that no other framework encompasses all the variables in the process. Thinking systemically allows the supervisor to see the group more clearly in relation to other systems that intersect with it, such as the agency environment, the family systems of its members, and the therapy and supervisory subsystems. It also allows the supervisor to see the many levels of process that are going on at one time, and to expand the repertory of interventions to be made available to the supervisee. Cybernetics tells us that the person who has the most choices in a given system controls the system (Ashby, 1964). This is called "the law of requisite variety." To have requisite variety in supervision, we must always have one more way to view the situation than we need. Any one way of appraising the situation, no matter how potent, should be countered or enhanced with at least one other perspective or interpretation. The minute we begin to delude ourselves that we have found *the* answer, we lose flexibility and power in the system. As Jean Houston put it, "any single lensing is the enemy" (Houston, 1982, p. 37).

A major difficulty for the group therapy supervisor is getting accurate data about the group. All forms used by the therapist to report on group proceedings — audio and video taping, process recordings, subjective reporting of the therapist, and even one-way mirror observation — lend their unique distortions to the process; but no type of presentation or individual opinion about the group should be considered wrong. At worst a therapist's recounting of the group is insufficient or idiosyncratic. Thinking systemically in supervision forces us to accept that there are many truths about the group, and they all "stand side by side" (Durkin, 1981, p. xvi).

Although she only applies it to individual therapy supervision, Alonso (1985) has proposed a developmental theory of supervision which can be applied to the supervision of group therapy as well. Alonso differentiates levels of clinical and personal adult development of supervisor and supervisee, and predicts the potential advantages and liabilities of various combinations of supervisor and trainee in the treatment of clients who are themselves at different developmental stages. While she does not use a systems approach, Alonso's model approaches the supervisory relationship as a subsystem which influences and is influenced by the therapist-client subsystem.

The area of psychotherapy supervision in which systems thinking has been fully integrated is family therapy. In family therapy we find the supervisor acknowledged openly as an integral part of the treatment process (Minuchin & Fishman, 1981). Family therapists often operate in teams with one or two therapists doing the therapy with the family and others doing live supervision by communicating to the therapists through telephones or earphones from behind the one way mirror. This kind of supervision makes explicit to all parties the presence of the supervisor(s) in the client-therapist-supervisory system and the interconnections among these subsystems. By contrast, in group therapy supervision, the supervisor is usually hidden from the rest of the system, except to the therapists during supervisory sessions. If the supervision of group therapy is to be effective, supervisors and group therapists must constantly be reminded of the phenomena of circularity, mutuality of influences, and the fact that a change in one area of the system will produce simultaneous changes in other areas (Nicholas, 1984).

For years organizational psychologists have applied a systems model to the understanding and management of supervisory functions in organizations. Such knowledge would seem just as crucial for the supervisors of group therapy, yet psychodynamically-trained group supervisors typically know little about organizational development or systems theory. Remarkably, even though as group therapists we espouse a group-as-a-whole perspective of group dynamics, when it comes to seeing the supervisor as a functional part of the larger group system, we tend to revert to a whole-equals-sum-of-the-parts way of thinking.

GROUP SUPERVISOR ENERGY
IN THE THERAPY GROUP SYSTEM

A therapy group with a supervisor is an organization with three major subsystems: the group, the therapist(s) and the supervisor(s). The most complex subsystem is the first, the group itself, which is a system of representatives from a great many other systems: social, familial, emotional, cognitive, and thematic. The function of a living system (all organizations are living systems) is to take in materials from its environment, transform them in some way, and export them back into the environment (Miller & Rice, 1975). A major nutrient that traverses through the boundaries of a living system and is utilized in the system is *energy*. A system that is taking in sufficient amounts of energy in a form available for work will utilize this energy in ways that automatically serve to enhance the differentiation and levels of organization of the system (Gruen, 1981). A system that does not receive enough usable energy will deteriorate into a disorganized state, known as *entropy*.

The therapy group system is an open system to which many sources of energy have access. The most obvious provider of energy to the group is the therapist. Less conspicuously, the group therapy supervisor is also an important source of energy to the group, this energy being infused into the therapist-group system through contact with the group therapist in the supervisory session.

Another basic principle in systems theory is that there exists an *isomorphy* (parallelism or identity) of structure and of self-organizing processes among living systems (Durkin, 1981). It is my belief that the kind of energy required by the group from the therapist at any given stage of the group's development is isomorphic with those needed by the therapist(s), a concept which conveniently narrows the field of supervisory interventions which might be appropriate at any given time. The art of "good enough supervising" (to coin a phrase from Winnicott) involves the selection and measured infusion of energy into the therapist(s) subsystem, the transformation of which will result in the appropriate kind of energizing of the group for its further growth and development. I will now offer some distinctions among kinds of energy offered by the group therapy supervisor to the supervisees at different group stages.

Nurturant Energy

Gruen (1981) sees the therapy group as a system of energy transformation, and claims that the therapist's nurturant energy is of vital importance to healthy group development. I think the concept of nurturant energy applies also to supervisory functions, particularly in the early stages of a group's development.

At its inception a group needs a great deal from the therapist. The therapist must work hard to screen, select, and prepare clients for the group. Keeping the group together until the starting gate and during the first several sessions requires great effort and is often quite difficult for the therapist to achieve. The therapist must make people feel welcome and hopeful about the usefulness of the group, be clear about expectations, and probably be more directive in helping people connect with one another than might be required later on. The supervisor at this early stage of the group gives the supervisee considerable practical suggestions and theoretical input. I see the processes of energy being provided by the therapist to the group and by the supervisor to the supervisee at this stage as being isomorphic. In both cases the energy being provided is highly nurturant. It is simple and digestible, transmitted in a manner that is comforting and building of security — a little like mother's milk or baby food.

A pair of Yale psychology graduate students, eager and green, had already started a mixed adult therapy group when I was asked by the director of their clinic to supervise them. The ebullience of these two inexperienced therapists far exceeded their knowledge of group treatment principles or methods. They had energy to burn which they lavished on their group. The result was a group with a very bumpy start. Terming the group "heterogeneous," they had admitted a man thirty-five years older than the next oldest member. This gentleman, whose name was John, had an officious and controlling personality which combined with his advanced age to propel him immediately into the role of father and grandfather in the group. He quickly made most of the members and the leaders angry at him. The intrepid co-therapists relished what they perceived as the healthy expression of conflict within the group. They were disillusioned and frustrated, however, when members started to drop out in the early weeks of the group, telling the leaders privately that they could not tolerate John.

I identified the problem with the way this group was beginning. While the group therapists' spontaneity and dedication gave inspiration to group members, their abundant energy was having detrimental rather than beneficial effects on the group. The group was not yet at a stage where it could utilize this energy. The expression of conflict and hostility was premature and divisive, and needed to be contained rather than encouraged. The leaders were providing fire and gasoline to the group, when what the group needed from them was sustenance and safety.

Our supervisory sessions, like the group sessions, were somewhat chaotic. The therapists seemed noisy and out of control. They were staying up all night after each group meeting transcribing the sessions practically word for word from their tapes and then trying to read me all of it, with no sense of how little time we had. They offered fairly loud and unreasoned comments and often laughed hysterically. I felt that while they idealized me, they were not listening to me. In a way it was like working with two little children who were overstimulated, and they were beginning to get on my nerves. I reasoned that if the therapists made me jittery, they might be having the same effect on the group. What they were pumping into the system was anxiety not nurturance. The therapists' energy was being wasted, and the larger system was in danger of deteriorating into entropy before it had a chance to organize itself.

Isomorphically, my supervision at this point needed to provide the therapists with what the group needed from them — a structuring nurturance. First, I calmed down the tone of the supervision sessions, slowing their presentation and chewing each point over carefully. I insisted that they read some specific books and articles about group therapy, and I interjected more theory into our analysis of their group. I helped them attend to inclusion criteria (external boundary) by reassigning the older man in an appropriate group. My final supervisor intervention during this stage was unconscious — I demonstrated the need for nurturing in the therapy group system by having the therapists to my house for lunch. The therapists settled down and became clearer and more thoughtful in supervision sessions, which translated immediately into the group becoming organized, stable and cohesive.

Fuel

While at the early stages of a group, the therapist and supervisor provide a nurturant energy, throughout the life of the group they provide a different kind of energy, one that can be likened to fuel. The fuel is of a few varieties, but many come under the heading of positive reinforcement. Positive reinforcement in the therapist-supervisor subsystem, although not obvious to the group members, is vital to the survival of the therapy group system as a whole.

Thinking systemically increases our awareness that positive reinforcement in the therapy group system is not a one-way street. Just as the therapist must receive gratification from running the group, the supervisor must receive positive reinforcement from her supervisees, and also be able to obtain satisfaction from the successes and learnings of group members that she hears about from the group therapist. Group supervisors who enjoy the task are apt to feel just as proud when things go well in the group they supervise as they do when they achieve some success in a group in which they are the group therapist.

Catalytic Energy

Some kinds of energy are not needed continuously in the therapy group system, but are required at certain times when particular functions of the system are lagging. This third kind of supervisory energy is catalytic energy. A catalyst is "an agent that provokes change or causes change in rate of reaction, without itself being essentially altered in the process" (Mendell, 1981, p. 128). Catalyzing a system gets it going in a certain direction. When a group is stuck, the group therapists try to intervene in some way that will remobilize its energies. Similarly, when the therapist-group subsystem is stuck, it may need a shot of energy from the supervisor.

When the group is demoralized, the therapists often become discouraged too. If all goes well, the supervisor at this point becomes a catalyst by injecting hope and a sense of humor about the situation. When the therapists become fearful in their role, the supervisor lends them courage. When the therapists are stuck in the way they view a situation, the supervisor offers them a fresh viewpoint. These are just a few examples of how the supervisor's energy is used to catalyze the therapist-group subsystem.

Karen, a thirty-five year old psychiatric nurse and a ten-year veteran group therapist at the state Mental Health Center was already in danger of burn-out, when she was assigned an outpatient group of chronic schizophrenic and brain-damaged individuals whose level of burn-out in life was comparable to hers as a therapist. She came to her first supervision session at my office with a polite look on her face that said, "Why don't you and I just face the fact that this is going to be boring, and I probably know a lot more about all this than you do." I responded to her highly competent presentation of the group with great respect and interest. Validating her obvious skills and dedication, I asked if she knew anything about psychodrama and sociometry. Her eyes widened. "No, but I'd like to!" she exclaimed, amazed at the possibility that one of her supervisors would actually teach her something practical and new. She eagerly put into practice the few techniques I gave her in the early stages of our work together. I invited Karen to join a peer supervision group that used psychodramatic role plays to explore the dynamics of the therapists' groups. She was excited to meet group therapists who were using creative therapy techniques and working in a variety of interesting settings.

Karen was quickly energized in supervision, and this immediately translated itself into her work with her schizophrenic group. She remained heartily enthusiastic about her group for the entire two years of its duration. While other aspects of her work were stressful, she reported that this group was consistently the high point of her week. The patients seemed to flourish in the group, with improved relationships and vocational success. The attendance of this group was excellent, and no one dropped out in the two-year history of the group.

Karen is highly skilled and may well have led a successful group without my assistance. It was not *what* I taught her that helped her recover from burn-out, rather it was the catalysis I generated at a time when she really needed it. By showing her that there was something new under the sun when she was deprived of or shutting herself off from new input, I was giving her a massive battery re-charge. She was then able to continue under her own power, which was considerable. To complete the energy circle, you may have gleaned that Karen is the kind of supervisee that catalyzes a supervisor. Not only did she respond immediately and positively to my input, but she made it a point to praise me to everybody at her agency. Karen's transformation of the energy I gave her resulted in my receiving energy back from her which fueled not only my relationship with her, but kept me going in more draining supervisory situations, such as the one with Jeff and Linda described below.

WHEN ENERGIES ARE BLOCKED OR MISDIRECTED

Sometimes the supervisor's energies are in the right form but are blocked and/or misdirected. The energy does not seem to flow in the right directions at the right time. This was the case in my supervision with two social workers, Jeff and Linda, who were leading a therapy group of fairly high-functioning adults in Jeff's private practice. At the time the group began, Jeff had been my co-therapist, supervisee, and best friend for eight years; and Linda had for several years been a client in a group that Jeff and I were then co-leading. This group ended about four months *after* Jeff and Linda's group began. When Jeff asked Linda to co-lead with him and me to supervise, I was surprised and dubious—but not dubious enough, for I accepted the offer. Love and unresolved idealizing transferences have been known to conquer reason and clinical judgment, and they certainly did in this case.

From the beginning of the group, I felt frustrated with Jeff and Linda. Listening to the tapes of their group therapy sessions, I thought both therapists sounded ponderous, unempathic and dull-witted, while in the other group, they had been spontaneous, sensitive and effective. In the supervision sessions, they seemed completely tuned out, while I felt myself working much too hard. I taught them theory and scoured journals for relevant articles for them to read. They expressed excitement about my ideas, but they never subscribed to group journals themselves nor attended conferences or workshops on group therapy. They rarely had hypotheses of their own about what was happening in the group, but would simply talk vaguely about their group sessions, usually without benefit of written records. When I gave them instructions (which I always knew was the wrong thing to do but I kept doing it anyway) they would robotically implement them — usually with poor results because their timing was off, or because they were not taking into account changes in the group since I gave the suggestions.

When I stated my distress about the functioning of the group and the supervision, they felt put down and criticized and became more passive. I felt guilty, and compulsively pumped more energy into the supervision sessions. We were stuck in a positive feedback loop (Gruen, 1981), where my input was generating passivity on their part, which would mobilize me to pour in more energy, thereby increasing their passivity once again, and so on. This spiral was rapidly depleting me and leading the system toward entropy, not to mention eroding the respect and camaraderie the three of us had once shared.

The threat to the group's survival that first year became fairly acute. Members were dropping out with only minor attempts to disguise their dissatisfaction with the group. Oddly, this did not seem to bother the therapists, an indication of how little invested they were in the group, although they claimed otherwise. One woman saw an individual therapist while attending the group for four months and never bothered to mention it to the group or the group therapists. When the therapists nonchalantly told me this, I was appalled. "Can you imagine someone going into individual therapy from the old group (Jeff's and my group in which Linda was a client) and not talking about it in group?" I asked. With a shock it dawned on them that if anyone had tried such a thing in that group, the person would have been confronted for weeks. At that point we all realized something was amiss. These therapists were far more competent and alive in other clinical situations than they were in this group. What was going on in the larger therapy group system context that could explain this anomaly?

The therapy group system was suffering from a situation in which energies were trapped in two of the subsystems in such a way that they could not be processed into energies that could be utilized by the group system. While Jeff and Linda took everything I said to heart and tortured themselves with it, they were not able to listen to their group. When they were not lapping up wisdom from me in supervision, they were trying to enlist me in their struggles with each other. Both the therapist subsystem and the therapist-supervisory subsystem were bogged down, with lots of energy going into these relationships, and little coming out that could be of benefit to the group.

After a year or more of all three of us feeling frustrated and impotent, we decided Jeff and Linda should have another supervisor. Interestingly, the new supervisor focused on a subsystem that the three of us had tended to overlook, the co-therapy team. He saw Jeff and Linda's prior relationship as therapist and client as the major log-jam in the system. Was Linda really on a par with Jeff or was she in a one-down position? Did she have as much impact on him as he did on her? Was Linda separate enough from the client subsystem to be useful to them? His probing questions mobilized Jeff's and Linda's energy, and they soon began to function more freely and use the competence they possessed, which naturally improved the functioning of the group.

Durkin (1981) says that the group therapist manages the flow of energy in the group system by interventions known as "boundarying functions." He says the group therapist must be "open to openness and closed to closedness" (p. 239). Whenever a door in communication opens between two members we try to keep it open, encouraging clients to say what they mean even at the risk of embarrassment or the other's displeasure. Pseudo-communication is that which might seem to provide a boundary opening, while it actually closes boundaries. An example is a client who requests the group's help, but then proceeds to talk to the wall, allowing no opportunity for others to respond.

Group therapists must be able to discriminate between openness and closedness, reinforcing the former and challenging the latter. When we empathize we let people in. We are "open" to their "openness," they are opening a boundary and letting out energy and we are taking it in and letting it affect us. When we confront others in the group with their conscious or unconscious attempts to deny, hide or lie, we are demonstrating that we will not condone closedness. My frustration with Jeff and Linda had centered on their routine acceptance of inauthentic transactions in the group, i.e., their openness to the group's closedness. Little did I realize that in supervision I had similarly left myself open to my supervisees' closedness. Instead of confronting their passivity, I wasted a lot of energy trying to compensate for their blocked spontaneity, which I could not do. I realize now that our collective motivation was probably to preserve our old group system at the expense of Jeff and Linda's group.

In time, with the new supervision, Jeff and Linda were able to liberate the energies that had been tied up in supervision and in the co-leadership, and infuse them into the new group where they belonged. Jeff and Linda were finally able to perform as an equal co-therapy team with the competence and enthusiasm I had expected all along. Our collegial and friendship relationships were gradually restored.

SUMMARY

Systems principles allow the group therapy supervisor a wide variety of frames of reference and techniques to apply to group treatment and supervision. The group supervisor, like the group therapist, must have a variety of different kinds of energy on tap to infuse into the group therapy system, and must be able to differentiate boundary situations which impede versus those which catalyze energy exchanges within the group. Generally, the kind of energy needed by the supervisees from the supervisor is similar in quality to the kind of energy needed by the group from its therapists at that particular stage in its development. Group therapists' and supervisors' manipulation of boundaries of the various subsystems of the therapy group system affects the flow and utilization of energy throughout the system. Further work on application of other systems concepts besides energy utilization to the supervision of group therapy should be pursued.

REFERENCES

Alonso, A. (1985). *The quiet profession*. New York: Macmillan Publishing Co.
Ashby, W. (1964). *Introduction to cybernetics*. New York: Science Paperbacks.
Durkin, J. (1981). Outside/inside/opening/closing: instructions for living groups. In J. Durkin (Ed.), *Living groups: Group psychotherapy and general systems theory*. New York: Brunner/Mazel, 228-253.
Gruen, W. (1981). Group therapy as a system of energy transformation. In J. Durkin (Ed.), *Living groups: Group psychotherapy and general systems theory*. New York: Brunner/Mazel, 79-97.
Haley, J. (1963). *Strategies of psychotherapy*. New York: Grune & Stratton.
Haley, J. (1973). *Uncommon therapy: The psychiatric techniques of Milton Erickson, M.D.* New York: Norton.
Houston, J. (1982). *The possible human*. Los Angeles: J.P. Tarcher, Inc.
Lankton, S. & Lankton, C. (1983). *The answer within: A clinical framework of Ericksonian hypnotherapy*. New York: Brunner/Mazel.
Mendell, D. (1981). Isomorphy in group therapy: The leader as catalyst and regulator. In J. Durkin (Ed.), *Living groups: Group psychotherapy and general systems theory*. New York: Brunner/Mazel, 127-144.
Miller, E. & Rice, A. (1975). Selections from *Systems of organization*. In A. Colman & H. Bexton (Eds.), *Group relations reader*. Sausalito: Colman & Bexton, 43-68.
Minuchin, S. & Fishman, H. (1981). *Family therapy techniques*. Cambridge, MA: Harvard University Press.
Nicholas, M. (1984). *Change in the context of group psychotherapy*. New York: Brunner/Mazel.
Watzlawick, P. (1967). *Pragmatics of human communication*. New York: Norton.
Watzlawick, P. (1974). *Change*. New York: Norton.

Chapter 3

Teaching Psychodrama:
A Workshop

Merle Cantor Goldberg

Under fluorescent lights, in an unfurnished room, two people move about tensely. The drama unfolding has no beginning and no end but moves backward and forward in time. Scenes change. Actors move in and out. An ashtray is hurled against a far wall; a woman sinks to the floor in tears. Perhaps a few quiet words are exchanged that have waited a long time to be expressed. This is not a written play but a recreation of a moment in one person's life. This is psychodrama.

THE EXPERIENCE

Workshop 4a Psychodrama:
Theory and Technique

This workshop is open to clinicians with more than four years of group psychotherapy experience (maximum registration 25). Chairperson: Merle Cantor Goldberg, MSW.

Merle Cantor Goldberg, MSW, is in private practice and is a nationally recognized group therapist. Inquiries may be addressed to 1107-A Spring Street, Silver Spring, MD 20910.

41

This workshop will present a brief didactic introduction to the theory of psychodrama followed by experiential group work utilizing various psychodrama warmup techniques. Included will be discussion and demonstration of the following techniques: guided fantasy, empty chair, and action sociogram warmups. Other techniques to be emphasized will be the use of doubling, role reversal, mirroring; the use of auxiliary egos and the importance of nonverbal communication. The aim of the workshop will be to acquaint the clinician with psychodrama and to teach the use of basic psychodrama tools that can enhance and deepen ongoing clinical work.

For all of you readers, welcome to workshop 4a for professional audiences in the United States and abroad. Most of the participants are experienced clinicians — primarily social workers, psychiatrists, and psychologists. Students also sometimes attend. Throughout the day there is a constant interplay between didactic content and action process. In this article I will move back and forth between content and process just as I do in the therapy session. And perhaps, like the participants in the workshop, you the reader may find yourself looking at behaviors in a slightly different dimension or, as J. L. Moreno, father of psychodrama suggests, with another eye. We'd better hurry; the workshop is about to begin.

Hello. I'm Merle Goldberg and we will be spending the next six hours together. I am a social worker in private practice in Washington, DC. My work includes traditional psychotherapy and Tavistock groups as well as psychodrama groups. Today I would like to share with you a set of theories and techniques that have added new possibilities and new dimensions to my clinical work. This is psychodrama, through the eyes of a psychodynamic therapist. I'd like to begin by asking each of you to tell a little about yourself — why you are here and what you would like to see happen for yourself in our time together.

After this brief introduction we move around the room, as the members talk about why they came and what they would like to see happen in our time together. I also talk about the resources I bring with me, tell a little about my background in the field, and discuss what I hope will take place today.

People come into a group with certain implicit and explicit expectations of what they want. In order to form an initial group contract we must find out what these expectations are. In most psychodynamic groups, we ask members to verbally state their expectations. Psychodrama, by contrast, relies heavily on nonverbal as well as verbal methods to ascertain group expectations. Therefore, I frequently begin my psychodrama workshops by inviting participants to try a brief nonverbal exercise. Let's go back to the group to dramatize this technique.

> Since psychodrama places strong emphasis on nonverbal communication let's begin by focusing nonverbally on how we are feeling at this moment in time. I would like the first person on my left to express the way he feels by taking a nonverbal body position to show his feelings. I would then like the next person to mimic his body position. In psychodrama this is called mirroring. Then turn in your chair and take your own body position.

Again we move through the group. Members slowly shift positions as they begin to consciously translate inner messages into overt body cues. They scrutinize the person on their right as they begin to mimic his or her body position. Perhaps, they begin to experience what the person on their right is feeling. Pairing, cohesion, and empathy, in a nonthreatening way, are all beginning to emerge. As they turn to their left, they can see a mirrored reflection of themselves.

> Let's begin to talk about what we have just experienced.
> — I'm not quite awake yet.
> — I am. I'm ready to go.
> — I didn't realize how tight my body was. Do I really look as angry as he mirrored me?
> — I felt so little and scared when I took her body position.
> — I guess I am scared.

The psychodrama warmup has begun.

For me as the leader, this exercise provides a quick indicator of some of the feelings in the group; it tells me who is actively involved and who is distant and shows the way members are beginning to relate to each other. It also gives me an initial sense of the comfort level of various members—in the ways they use their bodies as well as through their words.

This exercise is usually seen as fun for the group and arouses minimal initial anxiety even though it is, in reality, a way to immediately cut through words that can obscure feelings. It allows members to quickly make some contact with people on either side of them and gives every member a chance to participate; this makes later verbal participation somewhat easier.

We have completed our processing of the initial warmup exercise; I begin my didactic presentation. I now present a brief overview of the history and theory of psychodrama which will serve as a framework for the participants' later experience.

Psychodrama, developed originally by J.L. Moreno, has been defined as ". . . a method of psychotherapy in which the patient enacts meaningful experiences rather than simply talking about them. . . . [Psychodrama includes methods and ideas, such as] sociodrama, sociometry, role playing and a variety of techniques that can facilitate group processes" (Blatner, 1985, p. 3). In discussing psychodrama it is difficult to separate the method from its creator, Dr. Moreno, who defines psychodrama quite simply as the science that explores the truth by dramatic means (Moreno, 1953). Moreno began his acting out techniques by telling stories and then engaging in fantasy enactment and spontaneous play with children and their parents in the parks of Vienna. The concept of using this spontaneous enactment as a form of therapy did not emerge until later. After World War I, Moreno began a new theatrical experiment called the "Stegreiftheater," or theater of spontaneity, which he originally intended as a new form of entertainment. Moreno's group of professional entertainers would enact a drama on stage with improvised play, action, and dialogue, suggested by cues from the audience, newspaper headlines, or current events.

Although his theater began as entertainment, the deeper potentials of spontaneous acting began to take form for Moreno when he observed a particular young actress (Arieti, 1959). Barbara was a main attraction because of her excellence in playing ingenues and heroic and romantic roles. One day Barbara's husband George came to Moreno in desperation. Barbara was a "hellcat" at home and he felt entirely unable to deal with her. Moreno decided on a remedy. Convincing Barbara that she should broaden her range, Moreno cast her as a streetwalker whose recent death had made headlines. She played the role with such ferocity that at the climactic murder scene the audience stood up screaming "Stop!" At home after the show, Barbara was purged of all her aggressions and appeared extremely tender. Moreno kept her playing violent roles. Some months later, Barbara and George told Moreno they had "found themselves and each other." Moreno analyzed the development of their psychodrama and explained to them the story of their cure. This was the beginning of psychodrama.

At the same time the Stegreiftheater was developing, Moreno's first therapy clients included many prostitutes from the red light district of Vienna. Through his interactions with these women in organizing a self help group, he discovered the principle of the therapeutic agent: each member of the group can serve as the therapeutic agent for another, and the therapeutic nature of groups comes from interactions with one another rather than from the group leader (Buchanan, 1984). This was revolutionary thinking at this point in time.

In 1925, Moreno moved to the United States because he felt the country offered more freedom for the development of his ideas. Although there were innumerable advances made during these early years, a few bear special mention. In 1928, therapeutic role playing was introduced at Mt. Sinai Hospital; the following year, the impromptu theater, combining psychodrama and group dynamics, was offered at Carnegie Hall. In 1932, Moreno introduced the term "group psychotherapy" at an American Psychiatric Conference (see Blatner, 1985). In 1945, he founded his second journal later renamed Group Psychotherapy which became the official professional organ of the American Society for Group Psychotherapy and Psychodrama (ASGPP). What is most impressive is that these early publications by Moreno formed the foundation for group therapists 20-30 years later. A little known fact is that in the 1930s and 1940s,

Moreno's students included Fritz Perls, Eric Berne, Marion Chace, Theodore Sarbin, and Ronald Lippitt. Karl Menninger established a psychodrama theater in Topeka, and the editorial board and writers for the publications included John Dewey, Read Bain, Gardener Murphy, George Murdock, Margaret Mead, George Gallup, Adolf Maeyer, Kurt Lewin, and Rudolph Dreikurs — an impressive list.

With this background we might ask what exactly was it that Moreno was attempting to do. Certainly Moreno was helping people realize the potential of cure through spontaneous acting out and through interaction with peers. In the context of his time, the use of body involvement, drama, and peer interaction was a revolutionary concept. Moreno disagreed with the prevailing Freudian therapy because he felt it was impossible to reach into the mind of others to see what they thought and felt. Psychodrama, through controlled acting out, aims to make total behavior directly visible, observable, and measurable, and then to resubjectify, reorganize, and reintegrate that which has been objectified. Let's go back to the group now, to see how this applies.

Earlier we saw one nonverbal method of forming a group contract. In psychodrama we might also form a group contract in a different way by something called future projection through the use of guided fantasy. Let's try it. I'd like you all to sit back in your chairs, close your eyes and relax. Imagine you are entering a rocket ship moving through time and space. Grab a seat and hold on. We are about to take off. It's 11:00, 12:00, 2:00, 4:00, 5:00. The workshop is now completed and you are about to leave the room. Gather your belongings and head for the door, and as you reach the door realize that there is someone waiting for you — someone you really want to see. Greet that person and describe the day. Describe what you got from the experience and tell the person what you did not get. Imagine a detailed conversation. (Three minutes pass.) Begin to imagine what you did to keep you from getting what you wanted from the experience. The person you are with might help you with this by asking questions. (Two minutes pass.) Stay with the conversation another minute and then begin to say goodbye, knowing that at any moment you can close your eyes and go back to the conversation. In the meantime, the rocket ship is arriving again to take you back to Washington. Climb aboard. It's 5:00, 4:00, 2:00, 12:00, 11:00. The ship is arriving back in the room. Very slowly open your eyes and come back in the room. Who would like to begin by telling us about the experience?

At this point, members are asked to begin verbally sharing the images that have emerged from their guided fantasy. There is no set structure and unlike the initial warmups, I remain silent, waiting. Slowly, one by one, the group members begin to speak and relate to one another by questioning and free associating. They describe their significant other (the person they saw in the fantasy), their current concerns, their hopes, and fears. Even more significant, they describe their traditional patterns of resistance; behaviors that prevent them from getting what they want from the experience. For instance, a rather controlled-looking physician in a three piece suit stated, "I saw my wife. I told her that I was just going to sit back and take notes on what the other people were saying. I was not going to say anything at all because I knew it would be just as boring as the other workshops I've been to." In the process of describing the way his resistance was seen in the fantasy, his defenses begin to drop way. Through active participation, what also emerges with greater clarity is a new possibility for forming a group contract and thus a different way of answering the question, "What would you like to see happen today?"

The group members soon begin to focus on a topic, a central concern that many of the individuals seem to share. They begin by focusing on one of the individuals in the group. This is usually the individual who best personifies the central concern of the group. Today the group focuses on Mike, a man in his late thirties. Mike says he feels tired and burned out. Although he is having difficulty putting his feelings into words, other group members begin to relate to his comments and identify with him. Some talk of overload or dissatisfaction with their work. Others talk about a sense of loneliness, about decreased contact with friends and no time to spend with significant others. Someone expresses difficulty leaning on others, and someone else expresses sadness that there is no one in her life for her to lean on. Many members of the group feel that they give and give and get very little back. Since Mike's issues seem very relevant to the other group members, I ask him if he would like to be the protagonist and further explore what he is saying. He readily agrees.

During this period, I have served in a nondirective capacity, much as I would in my psychodynamic groups. As the individual who personifies this central concern emerges with some clarity, I begin to become more active again. We now move into the action portion of the psychodrama. In our theoretical group we might see the following action vignette.

Merri (to Mike): It is now 5:00 and the workshop is ending. Please begin to gather your things and walk toward the door. (Mike stands up as if gathering his things and moves towards the center of the room. I act as the director and move with him.) Who do you see standing there?
Mike: I see my wife, Jeanie.
Merri: Can you choose someone to play Jeanie?

Mike looks around the room and chooses someone to play his wife. Mike probably will choose a person dealing with many of the conflicts that his wife actually experiences.

Merri: Can you describe Jeanie for us? What does she look like? What is she wearing at this moment in time? What is the first thing that you notice about this woman that would tell you she is Jeanie?
Mike: She is about 30, medium height and weight. Kind of average looking. But the first thing I notice is her eyes — very warm and caring.
Merri: Let's walk around Jeanie and look at her from all sides.

Mike walks around Jeanie. At this point we want to begin to have the protagonist, Mike, move in space. As director, I move with him.

Merri: Is there anything else you notice?
Mike: She's seven months pregnant.

The woman playing Jeanie, called an auxiliary, places a rolled sweater as a prop under her skirt to appear pregnant. I file this fact for later use remembering that Mike's presenting problem is being tired and burned out. I begin to form initial hypotheses.

Merri: Can you begin to share the conversation?
Mike: Hi. I really missed you. I'm having trouble being here in DC. I'm so tired and can't seem to shift gears. I just can't seem to connect.
Merri: Reverse roles.

The initial role reversals are important since we are looking to have Mike role play his perception of Jeanie and not the auxiliary's countertransference.

Mike (as Jeanie): I don't feel like we've been connecting very much lately either. I'm kind of surprised you're telling me how you're feeling right now. What's wrong with you?//P*Merri (to Mike)*: Continue to reverse roles.
Mike: I don't know. I just feel burned out.
Mike (as Jeanie): Can you talk to me about what's wrong?
Mike: I'm having trouble putting it into words.
Merri: Would you like a double?

The double is a specialized auxiliary ego who stands behind Mike, takes his body position and expresses what he may be thinking and feeling but not saying. This helps Mike get in touch with his feelings by translating the body language cues that he might not be aware of into verbal cues.

Mike: Okay. (Double enters and stands behind Mike, taking his body position.)
Mike: I'm having trouble. I don't know what's wrong. I just feel so burned out.
Mike (as Jeanie): I know that you're busy but I need you.
Mike: I don't know what to say. I feel like screaming. I can't always be there for you. What do you want from me? (He raises his hands towards the sky as his shoulders sink.)
Double (taking Mike's body position and saying what he feels in that body position): I feel like I have the weight of the world on my shoulders.

Merri (to Mike): Can you give us an aside? (An aside means to turn your head so that other people don't hear and to express your feelings.)

Mike (aside): But I'll be okay. I've always taken care of myself and I can really handle anything.

Mike (to Jeanie): Yes, it feels like the weight of the world is on my shoulders. (His shoulders sink.)

Double: And it feels so heavy.

Mike: And it feels so heavy.

Auxiliary (as Jeanie): Maybe if you let me help . . . (pause) Can I hold you?

At this point the auxiliary playing Jeanie begins to take on the role herself and initiate the action.

Mike (coming close and letting Jeanie hold him, but remaining tense): I still feel like there is something between us. Like I still can't get close.

Merri cues the double.

Double: It's your stomach. You're seven months pregnant and your stomach is between us.

Auxiliary (as Jeanie): Do you think the baby gets in the way?

Mike: I guess I feel like it's so much more responsibility.

Double: And I don't even know if I really want it.

Mike (thoughtfully): No, I know that I really want it. It's just that I'm so scared.

Auxiliary (as Jeanie): Why haven't you told me how you felt?

Mike: Oh, I didn't want to alarm you. You have so much to worry about, and besides, I can handle it. (His body stiffens up and he clenches his fists.)

Double: The way I handle everything . . . alone.

Auxiliary (as Jeanie): But you don't need to handle it alone. I'm scared too, but we can deal with it together. I hate it so when you pull away. I'm here for you.

Mike: What should we do?

Merri (to Mike): Reverse roles.

By reversing roles, Mike must say what he perceives his wife would say and perhaps what he would like to have happen.

Mike (as Jeanie): Let's just talk as soon as you get home and let's keep talking. One of the things we'll talk about is the baby. We're both scared but we'll be okay if we handle it together.

Merri: Reverse roles, again.

Auxiliary (as Jeanie): I need you. And you need me.

Mike: It's so hard for me to talk about what's happening in me. I'm so used to taking care of everyone else. But it sure sounds good. (Long pause.)

Merri (to Mike): Can you begin to say goodbye?

Mike: I'll see you soon. I love you.

Auxiliary (as Jeanie): I love you too. (Jeanie initiates a hug and Mike quickly returns it.)

What we have just experienced is the movement in psychodrama from warmup into action. The group is a new one and has not yet developed trust or cohesion. Therefore, the action is kept in present time, in one scene, and with a minimum of auxiliary and director participation. Conflict has only superficially been explored and the director has made sure that closure of the scene has been complete. All of this serves to limit depth and intensity at this stage in group development. Nonetheless, many of the group members have identified strongly with the protagonist or the auxiliary and are sitting on the edge of their chairs.

We have now experienced the warmup and action stages; let's return to the group for the third part of the psychodrama, the sharing. Can the group pull their chairs a little closer? I'd like the group members to talk to Mike and Jeanie about their thoughts and feelings during the psychodrama.

Almost all of the group members participate with wide variation in the issues that emerge. As in the warmup, members begin to talk about their own burnout, but this time they also talk about significant others and what they (the participants) do to create distance. One member talks about his difficulties putting feelings into words. He reveals that he sometimes feels alone and wanted to scream at Mike, "Just spit it out." Others talk about difficulty depending on others. One woman states, "I know I have good friends in my life now. I've worked hard at it. But how do you learn to depend on others when no one has ever been there in the past?'' Other members identify with Jeanie. One woman begins to cry, saying to Jeanie, ''I just got a divorce. I only wish I had told him how I felt about his distancing and that we could have talked.'' The woman playing Jeanie surprises the group members by beginning to cry too, stating that in reality her husband is similar to Mike and she knows how Jeanie felt. She tells Mike how alone she feels. She also knows that she needs to go home and talk to her husband about what has happened in the psychodrama for her. One of the members tells us she is pregnant and scared. And not surprisingly, some of the members identify with the unborn child.

The sharing portion of the psychodrama is not an analysis but a sharing of what members thought and felt while they watched; the goal for the group members (audience) is identification and catharsis. The material that emerged provides the basis for working through in the group and provides (if this were an ongoing group) a direction for future sessions. The sharing also provides an anchor to bring the protagonist back into the group.

We have now experienced through our action vignette, the three parts of every psychodrama session: warmup, action, and sharing. The warmup and sharing portions of the drama are usually similar to the recreation described, but the action portion may be very different. In most psychotherapeutic psychodramas, the action has many parts and may move through time from the present (presenting problem) to the past (antecedents of behavior) to the future (role training or future projection) to the present again. There may be many auxiliaries, playing real or imagined people, living or dead.

In our brief psychodrama we have also seen the five tools of psychodrama: the director (Merri), the protagonist or star (Mike), the auxiliary ego (Jeanie), the audience, and the stage (which in this case was the middle of the room). We have also experienced the techniques of mirroring, role reversal, doubling, and aside. We have had a first hand look at the role of the psychodramatic group leader. As the session progressed we would have the opportunity to observe a variety of other techniques and have the chance to move into greater depth on some of the issues that emerged. Later in the session we would be able to look at the way these techniques could be integrated into the participants' practice settings. And, as 5:00

approached, I would be hoping that members had come to understand why a traditionally psychoanalytically trained, cynical and independent student of the '60s had come to gain so much admiration and appreciation for Dr. J. L. Moreno and his techniques.

KEY CONCEPTS
THAT HAVE INFLUENCED MY WORK

Throughout the years, four of Moreno's concepts and ideas have held particular significance for me. They are the concepts of (a) action and body involvement in the psychotherapeutic setting, (b) creativity/spontaneity, (c) hope, and (d) empathy. Although some of these ideas have gained popular acceptance and use today, it is quite extraordinary to remember that Moreno was writing about them between 1917 and 1940!

Action

My approach in psychodrama training, like the techniques it seeks to illustrate, is action oriented — learning through doing. Moreno felt strongly that the Freudian two dimensional couch was artificial and the use of verbal language was limiting. In my training sessions, I place strong emphasis on moving beyond the language of words. Emphasis is placed on active awareness of nonverbal cues and the use of signs and symbols. After the initial didactic training, participation is physical as well as verbal. Protagonists and auxiliaries are urged to move freely through space utilizing inanimate objects in the room as well as other people to create their dramas. Techniques are structured to elicit material that is of less breadth and scope than in patient groups and much of the work is done in the present time. Nonetheless, these techniques allow members of the training group to experience in a limited manner, what their patients will experience in therapy groups.

Through active participation, workshop members experience the rapid intensification of their own omnipotent-dependency fantasies; this can occur when there is a very intense, directive, action oriented psychodrama director/leader. They also experience, in a more intense way than any didactic verbal experience can teach, the rapid regression and ego boundary blurring that can take place when involvement occurs simultaneously on a nonverbal, physical, as well as verbal level. Thus the prime importance of the sharing component discussed earlier becomes clear as does the need for reestablishing ego boundaries and reorienting patients to the here and now and to the group. Most importantly, through the emphasis on nonverbal communication and action, I am teaching participants to go beyond the dimension of words.

Spontaneity/Creativity

For Moreno, spontaneity and creativity were central to the process of psychodrama and for healthy living. Although this concept is theoretically complex, one of its basic tenets is relatively straightforward — the ability to respond to whatever new situation emerges or to be able to create new and more productive responses to old situations. This involves the ability to be flexible, to experiment with new behaviors, to take risks, to look for positive creative outcomes, and to remain, when possible, non-judgmental about your own and others' behaviors.

The spontaneity of the psychodrama produces a high level of energy, activity, and personal involvement for the members as well as the leader. For me, this is in sharp contrast to the leadership role I assume in my psychodynamic or process groups. Because of my active involvement, I vigilantly maintain objective distance and ego boundaries and am aware of my own countertransferential issues.

Hope

The third basic concept is the instillation of hope as an agent of change in group psychotherapy. This, for Moreno, is interspersed with his Godhead theories, centering around his insight that we must shift our concept of God from a "He" God, through a "Thou" God, to an "I" God (Leveton, cited in Blatner, 1985). This involves a strong feeling that change can occur and that patients have an almost Godlike ability within themselves to make this change happen. In psychodramatic theory patients are taught not to analyze their dreams but to dream again and then to make the dreams come true. I have found in psychodrama that the combined use of action, a belief in creative spontaneity and the delighted curiosity of the therapist does indeed instill hope in the patient. It struck me for the first time as I wrote this paper that perhaps it is no coincidence that I chose the vignette that I did for this article. The theme that I chose emerges frequently in my training sessions. We as therapists feel periodically tired and burned out. Perhaps at those times we too need the instillation of hope.

Empathy

Finally, there is the concept of empathy. In his "Invitation to An Encounter," Moreno writes,

> A meeting of two: eye to eye, face to face
> And when you are near I will tear your eyes out
> And place them instead of mine,
> And you will tear my eyes out
> And place them instead of yours,
> And I will look at you with your eyes
> And you will look at me with mine.

> (Fox, 1987, p. 15)

In my psychodrama internship I became fascinated with the concept of empathy training. "I will look at you with your eyes." Could we train people to do that? I once thought I could define the quality that we call empathy, the elusive process of feeling into another human being. Why is it that as students things seem so clear and as experienced clinicians the lines blur? Psychodrama, more than any other technique I have observed, helps us sharpen our empathic skills through its use of role training, role reversal, doubling, and its strong emphasis on nonverbal communication. The heightened intensity of the empathic process which occurs in the psychodrama group simultaneously on a cognitive, feeling, and bodily level illustrates better than words, Moreno's concept of cure through interaction with others.

SUMMARY

I have invited you, the reader, to visit with me in Workshop 4a. The portion of the workshop that we observed gave us a glimpse of the participants and illustrated some of the basic psychodrama techniques. It presented an overview of psychodrama history and theory and a brief look at the role of the psychodrama leader in the beginning of a workshop group. I have described four of the concepts of psychodrama: active involvement, spontaneity and creativity, hopefulness, and empathy. These concepts serve as a continuing reminder for me that cure and personal growth comes through interaction with others. This has not only had a profound influence on my work but also on my view of mankind and on my life.

It's now five o'clock and time to end the group. I've enjoyed working with all of you today and I hope that in the future we'll meet again.

REFERENCES

Arieta, Silvano, ed. American Handbook of Psychiatry, Vol. 11, New York: Basic Books. 1959.

Blatner, Adam. Foundations of Psychodrama. San Marcos, TX: Adam Blatner, MD. 1985.

Bucanan, D. R. Psychodrama, in T. B. Karasu, MD (ed.) The Psychosocial Therapies: Part II of the Psychiatric Therapies. Washington, DC: American Psychiatric Association. 1984.

Fox, Jonathan, ed. The Essential Moreno. Writings on Psychodrama, Group Methods and Spontaneity by J. L. Moreno, MD. New York: Springer Publishing Company. 1987.

Goldberg, Merle Cantor. The Theory and Practice of Psychodrama. Ottawa, Canada: Canada's Mental Health. The Department of Health and Mental Welfare.

Goldberg, Carl and Goldberg, Merle Cantor. The Human Circle. Chicago: Nelson Hall Co. 1973.

Greenberg, Ira. Psychodrama. New York: Behavioral Publications. 1974.

Moreno, J. L. Who Shall Survive? Foundations of Sociometry, Group Psychotherapy and Sociodrama (2nd ed.). Beacon, NY: Beacon House. 1953.

Chapter 4

Circular Learning:
Teaching and Learning
Gestalt Therapy in Groups

Dorothy F. Napoli
Carol A. Walk

Gestalt therapy is taught in groups at the Cincinnati Gestalt Institute. This article will explain why and give a brief overview of the history of Gestalt therapy; it will provide some of the key principles, identify the therapeutic role, and discuss features of the Cincinnati Gestalt Institute training program.

The Cincinnati Gestalt Institute patterned and adapted its training model after the one started at the Gestalt Institute of Cleveland where the Cincinnati faculty trained as therapists. In Cleveland one of the training models focused on student groups in extended residence for the purpose of developing a knowledge base, practice, and personal growth. The rationale for using a group training model is consistent with the following Gestalt principle described by Joseph Zinker (1977):

> . . . growth takes place at the boundary between the individual and the environment. In other words, it is the encounter between what is me and what is not me which forces me to invent

Dorothy F. Napoli, ACSW, LISW, is in private practice and is Associate Professor of Social Work, University of Cincinnati.

Carol A. Walk, ACSW, LISW, is Co-Director of the Cincinnati Gestalt Institute and is in private practice. Inquiries may be addressed to 1302 Westminster, Cincinnati, OH 45229.

57

new responses for dealing with the environment and moves me toward change. The environment has an impact on me. And through this balance of assimilation and accommodation to a changing environment, I grow.

Gestalt group work emphasizes heightening the encounter and contact between individuals. (p. 163)

Although this does not imply training, it does infer learning. The Cincinnati Gestalt Institute bases its training program upon the idea that the individual grows as a result of contact with others (the environment). The boundary contact which occurs in groups nourishes and triggers creative processes. There are two Latin roots to the English word education, *educare*, which means to rear, to bring up, or to help another grow, and *educere* meaning to lead out. By integrating the Gestalt principle and these two Latin roots, group process can be utilized effectively in teaching and learning. This concept is our idea of circular learning. Circular learning then, is an educational process by which individuals learn and teach each other by doing and observing.

Students practice their work as therapists in the group and fellow students offer themselves as real-life clients to the therapists; others observe. Circular learning presumes that each contact with another student or faculty member while practicing or observing enlarges one's own boundary, and thus, enhances the creativity needed for application as a Gestalt therapist.

A metaphor for circular learning is the game of tennis. A player serves a ball across a well-defined boundary. The opponent returns the service according to the placement of the ball and the ability and skill at the return. In a good game of tennis each player's skills are stretched and enhanced by the skill and ability of the other player.

"Students" in this model must be able to risk self-disclosure as well as tolerate not-knowing in order to grow and develop. Alternatives about how to conduct therapeutic encounters in different ways are generated through the group interaction and individual examples as others respond in what seems to them to be new and innovative ways. Circular learning, then, is consistent with Gestalt principles of growth in groups.

HISTORY

Frederick Perls, a West German psychoanalytic psychiatrist is the founder of Gestalt Therapy. Perls became disenchanted with Freud's views of the unconscious and sex instinct theories as prime motivating factors in human behavior. In his first book, (1949), he outlined his divergent central concepts in the motivation of human behavior: need fulfillment, hunger instinct, and biological aggression. Among other things, he believed that needs organize perception which in turn motivates behavior.

Fritz, as he was commonly known, moved to New York City in the late 1940s and became involved with perceptual psychologists. He preferred the unified approach of body, mind, and fantasy, operating together to identify the perception of what is available in the environment to meet these needs and create unique coping mechanisms. In this way he began to work in what he called "the Here and Now"—helping people learn how to effectively meet their needs or make satisfactory contact in the environment. He combined his motivational theories with his work in perception into his second book (Perls, Hefferline, and Goodman, 1951). This was the first theoretical presentation of the theory of Gestalt therapy.

Fritz demonstrated his theory and style in workshops around the country, training other therapists in his approach. Since he was an outstanding showman, his work became well known. Others copied and mechanized his techniques without understanding the underpinnings of the theory; hence, Gestalt therapy gained the reputation of being "gimmicky." Far from tricks, however, he had developed methods of enabling people to identify their needs in the present.

Perls' methodology of helping people attain their potential for growth began with the idea that all organisms operate in their environment to maximize their own comfort. When an organism perceives a threat, the usual excitement that is available to act in the environment is turned into anxiety by constricting breathing and turning energy inward. This implosion of energy is an impasse which presents a barrier to the natural growth process at that point.

The uniqueness of Gestalt therapy that Perls developed is in designing an experiment that will heighten and explore the resistance to need meeting at the point of impasse. Within the safe environment of the therapeutic relationship, the person can explode the energy outward, coming through the impasse by acting and experiencing in new ways.

In the years since Perls' death in 1970, the theory has become more sophisticated and complete. The development of Gestalt Therapy continues today with such writers as Fagan and Shepherd, (1971); the Polsters, (1974); Zinker, (1977); and others.

WHAT IS GESTALT THERAPY?

Gestalt therapy (Perls, 1969) teaches the ability to attend to one's own processes in order to support the wholeness of the individual. Wholeness of mind and body working cooperatively to meet one's needs is a natural occurrence which operates effectively and economically unless some factor(s) in the environment impinges as a threat. If that threat is great enough and repetitious, we will perceive the environment as threatening even when it is not.

Factors which might present a chronic threat include spoken or unspoken family norms and rules that do not allow room for a child's unique expression of self. Thus a child develops a lasting or chronic resistance to certain behaviors which could otherwise lead to need-meeting. When need-meeting is not accomplished successfully, the individual repeats the behavior in an effort to find resolution; however, the resistance prevents the resolution.

Resistance, in Gestalt therapy, is understood as a behavior that at one time was a functional reaction to the environment. It is functional for a child to stop a feeling or behavior that is unacceptable to parents and that will bring noxious consequences. The child eventually learns to block the feeling or behavior at all times. This becomes chronic and removes the resistance behavior from awareness. The resistance is fixed, frozen, and repetitive, even when no longer functional.

Resistance often becomes lodged in the musculature of the body. It can be seen and/or experienced as frozen, rigid, or numb muscle groups. The theory of muscular repression in the body has its roots in Wilhelm Reich's (1949) concept of "character armor." At the point where the resistance is operating, new psychological growth does not take place. This is the point of impasse where Perls directed his therapy. He created a "safe emergency" in which the person could explore the resistance and explode the energy into behavior in the therapeutic environment rather than implode the energy in the form of anxiety, self criticism, immobilization, or some form of distortion of reality. New behavior or growth then can take place.

CYCLE OF EXPERIENCE

Good mental and emotional health in the Gestalt view is seen as the ability to move fluidly from sensation in the body, through awareness of needs into a mobilization of energy leading to need-meeting action. The action then results in contact with the environment, or within the intrapsychic environment, in such a way as to make contact that is fruitful and satisfying. The completion of this process leads to a natural withdrawal from contact to a period of rest and relaxation until the next cycle begins. This is a universal phenomenon in all human-kind in which needs are constantly occurring and being met. The Gestalt Institute of Cleveland has characterized this Cycle of Experience as shown in Figure 1.

This figure in the shape of a wheel describes the set of processes that direct behavior towards meeting one's needs. It begins with sensation and moves clock-wise to closure or withdrawal.

THE EXPERIMENT

The presence of resistance to movement through the Cycle is indicated by body language, voice, use of language, metaphor, fantasy, and dreams. The concept of the wholeness of mind and body are demonstrated here. What is going on in the mind is demonstrated by the body, and what is going on in the body organizes the perception of the mind. For example, one might hear constriction in the voice as though air is not being fully utilized to support the volume of voice or the throat is being constricted. The constriction is explored via an experiment designed by the therapist. The purpose is to discover perceptions which have organized the person's behavior into a pattern of resistance. One design might be to ask the client to tighten the throat muscles. The client would then be asked

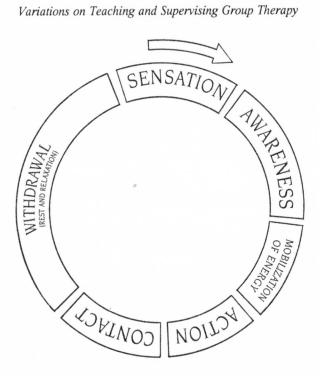

Fig. 1 Cycle of Experience

to stay aware and report any fantasies or images that occur. Often the client will become aware of parental injunctions which have forbidden the verbal expression of a class of feelings. The client has learned to cut off the expression of these feelings by chronic muscular repression. The experiment brings into awareness these ancient injunctions which are no longer necessary or useful in the "Here and Now."

The experiment is designed out of the interaction between the client, the behavior, and the creative processes of both client and therapist. As the client achieves greater awareness of the resistance and its meaning in current-day reality (the Here and Now), it then may be possible to experiment with new need-meeting behaviors in the safety of the therapeutic environment. In the above example, opening the muscles of the throat, breathing, and supporting self expression might be the content of the next experiment for practicing new behavior.

RESISTANCES

Resistances interrupt this Cycle at various places. The major resistances are desensitization, introjection, projection, retroflection, confluence, deflection, and holding on.

Desensitization is the process of depressing the inner excitation which allows one to notice sensation and awareness. In other words, the volume is turned down on the inner experience. It is not allowing oneself to experience feeling.

Introjection is the process of swallowing whole what is provided in the environment during the excitation phase of the Cycle. The information in the environment is not destructured and assimilated for discerning use by the individual. It often appears as injunctions or moral imperatives regarding behavior or feeling. An example of an introject might be, "You should never be rude." This may be a good rule of thumb until you find yourself victimized by someone who breaks in line in front of you. If you cannot ask the person to move, you are probably following a command you have swallowed whole without discriminating for yourself.

Projection is the process of disowning one's own experience and projecting it onto the environment where it is seen as an alien or undesirable feeling or behavior. This happens in the Cycle after the excitation is experienced and while energy is being mobilized for action. Its basis is in an introject in which the feelings or behavior has been forbidden. If the introject is that you should never be angry, you may disown your own angry feelings and instead, experience them as someone else's anger.

Retroflection is the process whereby the excitement and mobilization of energy are experienced but the action is turned inward against the self instead of out onto the environment. This can be seen as chronic self-criticism, psychosomatic illnesses, tension and pain in the musculature, petting, stroking or rubbing oneself, or even self-mutilation and suicide.

Confluence is the process of diminishing the appearance of differences between two or more people. It is an unaware contract between people who agree not to disagree. It provides the illusion of sameness while the people remain different. This occurs at the contract stage in the Cycle and results in diminishing the experience of uniqueness of the other. For example, when two people agree not to disagree both people have to watch Sunday afternoon football and one may not be enjoying it.

Deflection is the process of scattering or defocusing the action which defuses the power of the impact at contact. It, too, occurs at the contact stage in the Cycle. It has many different faces such as incongruity in effect and content, vagueness, minimization of feeling, over-specificity, or stereotypic expressions. An example of deflection might be smiling while one is expressing displeasure. The power of the emotion is diminished in this way.

Hanging-On is the process of not letting go of the contact after the satisfaction has been achieved. It prevents rest and relaxation as well as avoiding the vacuum which must occur to make room for the beginning of the next Cycle.

THE THERAPEUTIC ROLE

The therapist's role is to help clients gain a perspective on their needs, awareness, and behavior through monitoring the mind/body interaction in the present environment. The therapeutic task is one of monitoring the Cycle for chronic interruptions which then become the focal point of the therapeutic experiment. This therapy is an activity based process using experiment to explore resistance to need-meeting behavior. For example, a person talking blandly while shaking a fist exhibits incongruous behavior. Focusing awareness on bodily expression can help the client discover more about the needs and feelings that are being experienced at the moment. The bland voice is a resistance to the emotion demonstrated by the shaking fist. An experiment in the present might be to have the client talk about the anger in a monotone, heightening awareness of the incongruity between the two. The activity in heightening the awareness may trigger recall of parental injunctions against expressions of anger. Repeating these injunctions aloud brings to conscious awareness the rules of behavior the client is following. Expression of anger such as yelling, can be practiced as new behavior in a subsequent experiment.

THE TRAINING PROGRAM

The Cincinnati Gestalt Institute was designed nine years ago out of the faculty's interest in promoting a more humanistic approach to psychotherapy in a conservative community. It now provides a one year program with a three pronged thrust to teaching and learning the Gestalt approach. The program focuses on the learner's personal growth, theoretical knowledge, and practical experience. Thus the program offers three residential weekend retreats spaced at the beginning, middle and end of the academic year. Students focus on their personal growth work at these times. The faculty act as therapists in this therapeutic weekend group. In addition, there are nine monthly meetings of one full day. These meetings include a didactic presentation and the practicum experience. To compliment lecture material, students are expected to complete reading assignments prior to each session.[1]

Twelve students are selected for the program by a group interview screening process. Prospective students have an opportunity to get to know faculty and to see their interactions. The faculty assess the students' ego capacity to assure that they are able to move rapidly between the client, therapist, and observer roles to which they will be assigned. Consideration is given to the ability of students to work in these roles in front of a group. Facility in doing this requires ego strengths and boundaries to keep the roles clear.

Individuals from a variety of human service fields apply — social workers, psychologists, lawyers, ministers, nuns, physicians, art therapists. It is not a requirement that students wish to become Gestalt therapists, only that they wish to develop the Gestalt view of behavior and behavior growth.

In the past individuals with less than a bachelor's degree were admitted; however, their lack of psychological vocabulary and concepts hindered their learning. All students have been or are currently working in the field. This assures a basic knowledge of therapeutic practice.

PRACTICUM

A major distinction between this program and other therapeutic training programs is the structure of the practicum. Most practical training programs are designed on the tutorial model with an experienced therapist supervising and training the student/learner. That is not true in this training program. Here teaching and learning are done in groups.

The basis for this is the Gestalt concept that we know ourselves and others at the boundary point where contact is made. Contact at the boundary is where we can assimilate what is "not me" into boundary expansion. It is where the other can assimilate some of what "is me." Thus, trainer and trainee can incorporate and expand. This is our concept of circular learning. When we make contact, we change; when we change we give new input at the next contact boundary. Not only does the student learn, the faculty learns and returns that learning in a circular fashion at points of future contact.

Once a month there is a full day training session. The practicum is scheduled in the afternoon after the didactic presentation. The lecture is congruent with the task to be mastered in the afternoon practice session. The practicum is conceptualized on teaching/ learning the simplest to the most complex sequence of ideas and experience. Students start with the simplest task: learning to heighten sensation and awareness.

The sequence of sessions continue through identification of the resistances to teaching how to build an experiment and making appropriate contact. Session I, for example, emphasizes heightening awareness of bodily sensations in order to teach students to attend to raw sensory data and to provide an opportunity for students to tease out the areas of resistance to the process of contact. Sensation is the first and simplest concept taught and experienced. The other concepts covered in the lectures are theme, metaphor, fantasy, and dreams.

During each practicum session, the student is cast into three roles; that of client, therapist and observer. The twelve selected students are divided into three subgroups of four and each subgroup is assigned a faculty member for supervision. Four therapy sessions in each practicum allow each student the opportunity to be a therapist, client, and observer on a rotating basis. Students in the role of client are instructed to do their own personal growth work. Students in the role of therapist are given specific instructions to focus on the issues from the morning lecture material.

For instance, if the lecture material was on retroflection, the student as client would be instructed to identify any areas of tension or numbness within the body. The task of the student/therapist would be to apply theoretical concepts and guidelines provided by the faculty on how to "undo the retroflection." The specific manner in which the student applies the concept and guidelines is developed from the students' creative processes. The students' use of their own creative methods is a significant point of departure from the early mimicry of Perls' style. The faculty and the observer take specific notes on the application of the process. These are reported in the discussion following the exercise. Watching and discussing others' creative processes at work expands the boundaries of possibilities for all present.

The Student Therapist Role

Gestalt therapists do not present a blank screen against which clients' transferences may be projected. They are whole people who reveal their "Here and Now" feeling or fantasy information. Specifically, the therapists' feeling and fantasy self-information is revealed to clients to make a teaching or therapeutic point. At times, the therapist's images which occur as a result of interaction with the client in a therapeutic session may be shared as feedback to the client. For example, the therapist's image of the client as a turtle may be descriptive of the pace at which the client is talking at that moment.

Since a weekend of personal growth work has been held at the opening of the academic year, the faculty has some idea of the personal issues for each student. These personal issues influence the student's work as therapist. Students must access and use their own and their client's language of body, mind, and fantasy as part of the raw material in the therapeutic process. The students' same resistances to contact appear when in the role of client and of therapist.

If the student deflects intensity of contact chronically during personal growth work, it will probably be seen again as deflection from the client's processes during practice work as therapist.

The student/therapist job is to identify where in the Cycle of Experience the client is having difficulty. As the therapist monitors the client's movement through the Cycle, the therapist's movement through the Cycle is being monitored by the supervising faculty and observers. They are responsible for giving feedback to the student/therapist during the practicum work.

The other way the student's themes are identified and resolved is through the therapeutic process of the weekend retreats. As is consistent with theory of group development, the first retreat deals with issues of identity, power, and authority; work on personal issues is begun. The second retreat elicits intimacy; the core issues are moved closer to resolution. The third retreat deals with closure; the remainder of core issues is recognized and separation from the group is completed.

The Client Role

At no time in the practicum is the client given feedback. Only the therapist receives feedback in a factual observable behavioral language designed to promote learning and preserve the individual's dignity. Instructions to clients are merely, "do your own work. No one will be evaluating you." The process of being clients, that is, experiencing the Gestalt therapeutic approach to material of their own election, replicates that of actual clients. In the process of becoming a Gestalt therapist, it is necessary to experience this role to increase awareness and empathy.

The Observer Role

The observer role is structured to help students focus on the themes of the student/therapist. Therapists can organize their feedback by designating each observer to attend to each of the therapist's different thematic behavior patterns. The object of the observer role, while devised to give feedback to the therapist, also plays an important personal function. It allows the observer to step outside the therapist's shoes, to detach from the immediacy of involvement and interaction, and to take a moment to reflect. Observers are able to think about what they saw, what happened, and what might be developed as alternatives from their own creative processes.

The value of the observer role is that it allows the student to experience and heighten the ability to produce that moment of creativity that will be called forth in the instant when it is essential in therapy. As the student/therapist is working, the observers can develop creative approaches in their fantasy to what they are seeing. This creativity, which is the hallmark of the Gestalt therapist is more spontaneous without the pressure of performance in the therapeutic role.

There is also enormous value in observing others' creative functioning. It may trigger more possibilities for the student/observer. It is true here that the whole is greater than the sum of its parts. So the opportunity to reflect coupled with subsequent discussion within the group serves to highlight for the group the creativity of each member. This circular learning increases the opportunity for learning geometrically as each member of the group becomes teacher for one another, a decided advantage over the straight forward pedagogical classroom model where the students' primary source of learning is the instructor.

One task of the faculty is to assist the group in its quest for cohesion, a process necessary for optimal teaching and learning. Another task is to establish the learning goals and the climate in which both are assured.

SUMMARY

Circular learning is the educational and training model used by the Cincinnati Gestalt Institute to teach groups of practitioners the experience, understanding, and use of the Gestalt therapeutic approach within their own practice. Interaction and encounter of students and faculty expand the creative boundaries of each person in the group. The knowledge base is provided through lectures. Practical experience is gained by working as therapists before the observing group members and faculty. The observer role in this circular learning process increases the development of broader personal boundaries. Observations are contributed and lead to the expansion of the boundaries of others. The experiential personal growth work which takes place both during weekend retreats and practicum sessions supplies an additional perspective. In this model practitioners and faculty teach each other from within their own originality and creativity, and they both learn new ways of knowing and doing.

NOTE

1. The list of reading texts are: Frederick Perls, *Ego, Hunger and Aggression* and *Gestalt Therapy Verbatim*;Frederick Perls, Ralph Hefferline and Paul Goodman, *Gestalt Therapy: Excitement and Growth in the Human Personality*; Miriam and Erving Polster, *Gestalt Therapy Integrated*; and Joseph Zinker, *Creative Process in Gestalt Therapy* (see References for publishing information).

REFERENCES

Fagan, Joen, and Shepherd, Irma Lee, eds. *Gestalt Therapy Now*. Harper and Row, New York, 1971.

Perls, Frederick. *Ego, Hunger and Aggression*. Vintage Books, New York, 1949.

Perls, Frederick. *Gestalt Therapy Verbatim*. Real People Press, Moab, Utah, 1969.

Perls, Frederick, Hefferline, Ralph, and Goodman, Paul. *Gestalt Therapy: Excitement and Growth in the Human Personality*. Dell Publishing Company, New York, 1951.

Polster, Miriam, and Polster, Erving. Gestalt Therapy Integrated. Vintage Books, New York, 1974.

Reich, Wilhelm. *Character Analysis*. Orgone Institute Press, New York, 1949.

Zinker, Joseph. *Creative Process in Gestalt Therapy*. Vintage Books, New York, 1977.

Chapter 5

Teaching Transactional Analysis and Redecision Therapy

Robert Goulding

I have been asked to write a chapter on how I teach Transactional Analysis. Ninety percent of my work during the past 20 years has been teaching therapists. My form of teaching is to provide Transactional Analysis in intensive short-term group therapy. I only see people in training, not in therapy.

Transactional Analysis (hereafter referred to as TA) is a theory of personality and a systematic psychotherapy, first developed by Eric Berne in the late '50s. The basic concept is that each of us is made up of three parts: Parent, Adult, and Child. The Parent is a set of Ego States borrowed from real and surrogate parents; the Adult is our reality testing part; and the Child Ego States are repetitions of feelings and behaviors from our past. The original TA theory primarily identifies Ego States, analyzes transactions between one's own Ego States and those of others, and analyzes games and life scripts. A game is a series of transactions between one's own Ego States and/or those of others that end up in personal misfortune and/or unhappy feelings. The script is a life plan formed in childhood and lived on in adult years.[1]

Transactional Analysis has been a recognized treatment modality for 30 years. However, it may not be a well known fact that there are three schools of TA: the Classic, the Cathexis, and the Redeci-

Robert Goulding, MD, is Co-Director of the Western Institute for Group and Family Therapy. Inquiries may be addressed to 262 Gaffey Road, Watsonville, CA 96706.

sion Schools. The Classic School is represented in the work of Eric Berne (1961, 1964). The Cathexis school teaches reparenting of the patient by the therapist or therapist-surrogates. The Redecision Therapy School, established by Mary Goulding and myself, uses Transactional Analysis developmental theory but varies largely in the clinical approach. The basic theoretical position of Redecision TA is that all children, regardless of the nature of their stresses, make decisions for themselves about their thinking, behavior, and feeling, and perhaps about their body functions and symptoms. Thus, our belief is that in order to effect change one must get the clients to affectively change their early decisions (Goulding and Goulding, 1977). Thus we use gestalt, psychodrama, and any other modality that deals with affective work, or in TA terms, engages the Child Ego State in the redecision.

KEY TERMS

I use a series of short organized terms to teach my method of thinking and to plan the therapeutic thrust; I keep this organization in the back of my mind while working. These can be listed as follows and will constitute the headings of the subsequent paragraphs.

1. Contact
2. Clinical presentation of the patient
3. Contract
4. Cons
5. Chief bad feelings, thinkings, behaviors, psychosomatic body changes
6. Chief games, fantasies, belief systems that maintain those bad feelings, thinkings, behaviors, psychosomatic body changes
7. Childhood early decisions
8. Chief parental messages: injunctions, counter-injunctions, information
9. Childhood script formation and stroking patterns
10. Nature of impasse
11. Resolution of impasse in the work
12. Anchoring and changing stroke patterns

13. Plan for the future

CONTACT

There must be a starting contact when the patient and the therapist first get together when bonding can begin. I answer my own phone, write my own letters, greet the client personally, present an attractive physical setting (our ranch is on 70 acres of land on a beautiful mountain in California overlooking Monterey Bay and the surrounding moraine). Thus the patient, who lives here for a week to a month or more, begins to recognize me as an interesting human being, not an answering machine and/or a receptionist in a sterile office. During the initial contact, I also begin to look for physical and behavioral presentations that may be developed in the contract.

CLINICAL PRESENTATION OF THE PATIENT

How does the patient present himself/herself? Is he too fat, too skinny, obviously under the influence of drugs or alcohol, showing signs of cardiac disease, such as hypertension, cyanosis? Is she obviously depressed, scared, tremulous? Does he show signs of physical violence? Are the eyes crossed, is there stammering? It is quite possible that although there may be an obvious problem to me, the patient may not present this as part of the contract, and it will be up to me to confront this. For instance, I may tell a 300 pound hypertensive that I am curious why he wants to resolve his fears of intimacy when he is killing himself overeating!

CONTRACT

The contract must be specific, reasonable, measurable, and possible, not just exploratory. The question I ask is, "What do you want to change about yourself today (this week, this month)?" I do *not* ask such questions as "What is your problem?" or "What can I do for you?" I stress that the client is involved in the process, that change is possible, and that change is possible in the foreseeable future. I do not ask "What do you want to work on?", because a person could work on and on and on and not change. Thus, the question about "you changing today" avoids most of the possible cons (see below). Also, I do not accept what we call parental contracts. This is when a patient, smelling like a gin factory, states he wants to quit drinking. He is probably there because a spouse, child, parent, boss wants the change. There is a part of everyone who wants to change, but there is also a part of everyone who does not. This is called the adapted Child. It is this part of people that will try to con both themselves and the therapist.

CONS

All Americans know what a con man is. We have some difficulty in presenting this concept to the Japanese and other Asiatics, the Europeans, the Middle and Near Eastern peoples because the word "con" is not a part of their culture. In Redecision Therapy, we usually define the word as a process in which the person cons the therapist into agreeing that he will not do what he tells us he is going to do. For instance, the patient says "I'll try to do . . ." The therapist who accepts that essentially is stroking the patient. So the person continues to use words such as "try" rather than "do" and "can't" rather than "won't." The therapist/trainer has to listen very carefully for all these words and confront them immediately. "Are you going to try to quit drinking or are you going to do it?" "Do you mean you can't quit smoking or you won't quit?" There are not many things that we cannot do in the concept of a contract; there are many things, though, that people will not do.

Other things that we pay close attention to are body positions and body movements, particularly when they are incongruous. For instance, a patient says yes with her mouth while shaking her head no. We may ask her to say "no" aloud and see what happens, or we may ask her to nod her head "yes" while saying yes again. When patients are silent, they may be thinking things that end in scratching or picking on fingers, that may be very relevant to their contract. We will ask what is happening. A curious sign in English speaking people is the finger to the nose which almost always indicates suppressed anger.[2] This is particularly useful to note as an indication that a person is denying anger. It is also funny!

CHIEF BAD FEELINGS, THINKINGS, BEHAVIORS, PSYCHOSOMATIC SYMPTOMS

Most people who come to see a therapist have a primary set of feelings that many TA therapists call "rackets." I personally do not like that word, although it is part of the "cowboy" talk that Berne liked to use. These feelings, behaviors, and psychosomatic symptoms will be demonstrated, of course, in the working through of the contact, the contract, and the cons. I want to know specifically what are these feelings that the patient intends to change. I am not interested in "I want to know myself better," or "I want a peak experience," or "I want my spouse to change." Some people come to a therapist presenting physical symptoms such as headaches, backaches, or abdominal pains which may be psychosomatic. We are willing to work with whatever part of these aches and pains may be psychological. Now these symptoms, bad feelings (anger, depression, anxiety), obsessive thoughts, compulsive behavior, or somatic complaints are supported in their pathology by a series of events listed as chronic games, belief systems, and fantasies.

CHRONIC GAMES, BELIEF SYSTEMS, FANTASIES

These games, beliefs and fantasies allow people to feel bad. Feelings do not come out of the blue; people do not make us feel badly, think badly, behave badly. We have to do something to feel bad. "Make feel" simply does not exist in our work. To hear a group therapist say, "And how does that make the group feel?" makes my skin crawl. Please note the absurdity of my statement; I am responsible for my skin crawling because my belief system is that we are all basically autonomous. Part of our work is to teach people to be autonomous, not victims. So we teach people to be responsible for themselves and to give up their game playing, absurd belief system, and their unpleasant fantasies such as worrying (M. Goulding, in press).

What do I mean by a belief system? In the eastern Mediterranean area, a common saying and belief is that if one feels too good, something bad will happen. At a workshop we did there once, an Israeli was for a moment overjoyed after giving up her water phobia, and then she started to cry. When asked what she was doing, she answered, "I don't dare feel too good or my son will be killed in the war." Many people are so contaminated with this type of thinking they do not realize that what they think of as fact is only a belief system. All belief systems and games *must* be confronted.

CHILDHOOD EARLY DECISIONS

As the work progresses, I listen for ways I can facilitate the patient getting into the Child Ego State, using a real scene from the past. For instance, someone plays a game of "kick me" with me. At the end, whether he gets kicked by me or not, he will probably feel so. I confronted a therapist recently with his unwillingness to pay on time at a training workshop. The rules were laid down carefully. He was aware of them. Yet he "forgot" to bring his checkbook; he wanted to pay later, to mail his check when he returned home. He was both furious and hurt that I would confront him in front of the other group members. First I asked what he was feeling; I asked what he silently said to himself about himself. He had the following thoughts: "I am always getting picked on. I'm hurt. What did you say about me? How come you always pick on me. I'm mad at you."

I asked, "When you are a little kid and you get hurt and are mad at people and money is involved, what is the scene?" He then remembers that when he was a little boy, he was frequently being fined part of his allowance when he did not do something on time.

By giving clients three or more clues of their feelings, their behaviors, their thinking, and by using their exact words clients almost never fail to go back to an early scene. We use all present tense words, such as, "When you are a little kid . . ." or "What are you feeling . . ." in order to facilitate Child Ego State work.

In my early years with TA, I recognized that when I tried to get early scenes, the patients frequently could not remember. This is almost always true when a therapist asks for the "first scene." Most people cannot remember the first scene; actually, we do not need it anyway. Any good screen memory will achieve the same purpose. The clues we get circumvent the resistance and by using the person's exact words, we apparently stimulate the memory of an unclosed and unfinished gestalt. We are thus stimulating the same neurophysiologic pathways that were operating so that patients keep trying to solve the problem by repeating it over and over again, hoping to get the other person to change. Therapists must be ever vigilant and confrontive if they do not want to be conned.

CHIEF PARENTAL MESSAGES

For a prolonged description of the injunctions from the Child of the parent and the counter-injunctions from the Parent of the parent, read *Changing Lives* (Goulding & Goulding, 1977). In brief, parents give many irrational injunctions, demands if you wish, out of their own pain, suffering, and anger, which we theorize are from their own Child Ego State. They give many cultural messages from their Parent Ego State, such as "work hard." Any message can be dangerous if followed irrationally and obediently for the sole purpose of gaining strokes. Often these messages can be recognized by the way in which a patient changes from the first to the second person in the middle of a sentence. For example, commenting on her own fatigue, Carol. a therapist/patient, said, "I'm so tired; you work so hard and you don't have any fun." The change from I to you indicated that we are now listening to parental demands from a depressed mother: "Work hard and don't have fun." This gives us an immediate clue to the parent messages and to the early decisions the woman made to work hard, to not have fun, and to not be a child. Thus, early in life Carol forms her script to be a psychotherapist, to cure Mommy, to work hard, and to always be grown up. Then she will get many strokes.

CHILDHOOD SCRIPT FORMATION
AND STROKING PATTERNS

As indicated above, it is our theoretical position that the child formulates the script. In the early days of the old San Francisco Social Psychiatry Seminars, it was thought that the life script was inserted like an electrode into the child's head. It has long been our position that the child decides the script, based upon the messages received from parents and from the strokes received. If a youngster gets messages not to act like a child—to work hard carrying out the garbage, doing the dishes, even straining at bowel movements—if she gets strokes for working and for not acting childlike, then of course she will decide over and over again to comply. As a teenager, she may rebel, but this is an adapted rebellion and is still a response to the parents. This distinction is important because the work to be done is to channel her energy into free choices rather than into adaptive rebellion.

By adulthood, the script has already been formed and the stroke patterns established; it is very difficult to facilitate change purely on adult recognition of the script. The Catharsis School believes that the patient cannot change until permission is granted by new parents. In Redecision, we believe that people can reparent themselves in order to give up the script; they can stroke themselves and gather strokes from others who can support the change. It is important for the therapist to recognize this difference. It is difficult to teach autonomy if one behaves as if the patient is not autonomous. In our opinion, this is what reparenting does. Many of the classical TA therapists like to develop an elaborate script with an attempt to understand all the moves, as if the script were in a sense part of a recognizable fairy tale, like Cinderella. They spend much time attempting to determine all the characters, the patient's wicked stepmother, step-sisters, the pumpkin. This is an interesting exercise, but in our opinion wastes much time in the therapeutic encounter. The flow of the script is important, recognizing the stroke patterns are important, but elaborate definition is not. What is important for us is a rapid recognition of the Impasse, and the work designed to reach a resolution of that impasse.

NATURE OF IMPASSES

Our work is designed to recognize the impasses and to lead the patient to resolve each one. What is the stuck place? No matter whether the patient is anxious, neurotic, depressed, schizophrenic, or borderline, there are stuck places and they are reasonably defined. Carol, mentioned above, wants to quit working so hard and to have fun, to be childlike when appropriate, and not to cure all Mommies compulsively. She wants to, but she has great difficulty in doing so except rebelliously. She has at least two impasses: one, the problem with working hard; two, the problem with having fun. These two impasses are different: the one regarding "work hard" is what we define as Type 1 in which the messages are out in the open; the impasse regarding fun is defined as Type 2. It is harder to get at because it is covert.

The third type impasse is related to attributes with which the patient was born. In one family, the first child was the industrious one, the second the cute one, the third the stupid one. None of the children was really born industrious, or cute, or stupid; each one was tagged with these attributes by parents, siblings, others. It is important to recognize the difference between the three types because the treatment techniques are very different. Type 1 is involved with counter-injunctions from the Parent of the parent; type 2 with injunctions from the Child of the parent; and Type 3 with the attributes.

RESOLUTION OF THE IMPASSE IN THE WORK

Now comes the real fun, the real enjoyment. Up to this point the work has been designed to make contact; to be aware of patient differences; to make a workable contract; to tease out the chronic feelings, thoughts, behaviors; to tease out the games, fantasies, belief systems; to discover the nature of the impasse; and to keep reminding the patient of his or her autonomy by confrontation of the cons.

We have been doing the work in the present tense, in the here and now, in the I-Thou; the patient has not been allowed to talk about the past but must act out the past. For instance, if Carol wants to talk about her mother's depression, we put a chair in front of her and say, often in the words of the immortal Fritz Perls (the father of Gestalt Therapy), "Tell theese [sic] to her." If Carol wants to talk about her supervisor's unfairness about work demands, we say, "Tell theese to him!" The confrontations have been done humorously, with respect for the resistant and adaptive Child, but done consistently. She is not a villain; her cons are not malignant. She is a victim of her own parental injunctions but only as long as she allows herself to be. Now, she must face these injunctions, and we help her do so with gestalt techniques.

We may get her into past scenes, if this is done off of her energy and not ours. For instance, if we ask her to talk to her mother about her mother's depression and we find she is getting into a past scene, we may use this scene. Or, if she has been talking about her supervisor's "unfairness" we may go from that to talking to the supervisor, then to asking her how she feels, what she says in her head about him and about herself, and then we may go into the past by the three clue techniques described above.

Type 1

In a Type 1 impasse, the task is to counter the injunction from the Parent of the parent. As Carol resolves her impasse about working hard, she sees that she has used the supervisor to keep her there. Remember, people hold on to their bad feelings, use the world around them to blame, and then magically hope to find someone that will change. Actually, it is the parents they hope to magically change. If Carol has stayed angry at or depressed about her supervisor, magically hoping he will change, we can use this energy to explain to her "mother" in a second chair, that she is going to stay angry at "mother" until the real mother changes in the past. The absurdity of this is usually obvious and Carol was able to tell "mother" in the chair that she will no longer work hard for mother; she will only work hard when she wants to work hard. This redecision gets her out of the victim position as long as it is made from the Child Ego State. It is not sufficient to make it from adult recognition which still leaves the Child adaptive and self-sabotaging. She cognitively may say, "I'm not going to work so hard any more," and the Child will secretly say, "Hey, I've been getting all these strokes all these years for working hard; to hell with you!" Carol continues to work hard while blaming and being angry and also secretly rebelling by being late with reports, missing appointments, setting herself up to be told to work harder.

Type 2

This then is an example of the resolution of the Type 1 impasse. The work is out front; patients easily remember the words mother (or father) used, and the scenes so it is usually not necessary to do any "tricky" work. With the Type 2 impasse, the injunction is from the Child of the parent. With Carol, the impasse is her inability to have fun, her not being able to be childlike. Treatment may be easy or it may be difficult. She may quite easily tell "mother" in the second chair, "You never teach me how to have fun; you never allow me to have fun. I'm going out and find someone else to play with." We may then have her skip out of the room.

On the other hand, it may not be this simple. We may have to do a Parent interview in which we put Carol in mother's chair and ask her questions. Very often people have information that can be obtained from the Parent Ego State, information which is not immediately available to the Adult. Freud called this the unconscious or the subconscious. We find that this information is usually easily available by simply getting people into the parent Ego State and interviewing them. The questions may be very simple.

— What's your name, Mother?
— How old are you when she (patient) is five? What is happening in your life?
— Is it hard for you to have fun?
— Don't you want your daughter to enjoy life? How come you make her work so hard?

The answers to these questions may facilitate the redecision more easily. For instance, if Mother is chronically depressed, works hard to make a living, is a victim of Father's alcoholism, Carol can then make a free redecision for herself. She can empathize with mother rather than make a rebellious but adaptive decision against mother's demands. By definition, a Redecision must be made from the free Child Ego State. It must not be an adaptive rebellion against mother nor an adaptive compliance to please the therapist.

Type 3

In a Type 3 impasse, dealing with attributes, the problem is the patient's unawareness of any parental messages. There is no one to talk to in the second chair. In the case mentioned above, with the first child industrious, the second child cute, and the third child stupid, there were no clear messages. All Al remembers is having always felt stupid because he is certain he is stupid.

Here we use two chairs in the center of the room—one for the stupid (adaptive) child, one for the not-stupid (free) Child. We conduct not an I-Thou dialogue but a double I-I monologue. From the "stupid" chair Al describes his stupidity—difficulty at school, low tests in the army, etc. We then move him to the second, non-stupid chair and ask him to describe one time as a child when he felt normal or smart. We ask him to claim this. We then send him back to the "stupid" chair where he will probably disclaim it. We will continue this exercise four or five times. While he is in the first chair, we ask how he can be so stupid if he has a job as a counselor in a drug-alcohol clinic. He may grin and say "because I'm an alcoholic and they need alcoholics for that job." We then move him to the second chair and ask him to describe a smart thing he has done as a counselor. At some point Al will give up, as the energy flow decreases in the stupid chair, increases in the second, non-stupid chair. After all, a part of him knows he is not stupid and that is the part we are looking to stroke. Sometimes he may finally start to talk to "you," in which case we may switch to Type 2 work. The "you" just might be the patient's error, in which he forgets he is in an I-I monologue. There are not two Children; the patient's Child is Adaptive when he is listening and responding to internal or external parents; he is Free when he is not under parental influence.

More About Impasses

Let me add a few more words about impasses. Actually, the type of impasse does not relate to severity or difficulty. Sometimes a Type 1 is very difficult and often a Type 3 is very easy. In my previous writings (Goulding & Goulding, 1978, 1979), I described them as first, second, and third degree rather than Type 1, 2, and 3. However, I changed the labels since many TA therapists confused this with Berne's description of first, second, or third degree Games, which do relate to severity.

Not all impasses are solved by gestalt/TA work. Many phobic impasses are solved by desensitization procedures, for instance. I desensitize height phobics by fantasy work, first seeing themselves climbing a ladder or a cliff; then by using a real ladder against our barn (once, in Germany, against a church wall). Rather than use Wolpe's relaxation techniques, I use humor to elicit the Free Child taking over—redeciding as he or she laughs. I use actual pool work with water phobics, taking them into the pool, holding them in my arms to facilitate their floating. I do no prior fantasy work because they cannot imagine themselves floating. Working with water phobics is fun—for them and for me. They laugh as they begin to float and the feeling I have of their body beginning to relax is glorious.

We do not always have to go into the past. Many impasses are resolved in the present with present day experiences, as long as the Free Child is doing the work. Humor is a good way to get him to do that; what Jim Simkin called "organismic disgust" is another. Here, a "stupid" player with a Type 3 impasse may give it up as he exaggerates his stupidity to the rest of the group.

Working with headaches and other psychosomatic illnesses is usually fun and gratifying. We ask the patient with the headache (he must be having one at the moment) to put his hands to his head where the headache is dwelling. Once he has done this, we ask him to put the headache dramatically on the chair we have placed in front of him. He does so; if not dramatically enough, we ask him to do so even more vigorously. (We are beginning to cathect the fun Child.) Then we ask him to talk to his headache. Often he will start out with a whining, "I wish you would go away." We keep asking him to take more charge, until he is willing to be autonomous. Then we ask him to take the other chair and be the headache and respond. We keep this exchange going with short statements from each side. Taking the headache side, most patients become more energetic at first and may respond with statements like, "You need me; you are not getting rid of me." Then the response begins to become more energetic from the first chair as the patient says, "I don't need you; what do you think I need you for?" Now, whatever the response from the headache, the patient can take charge and fight back against his adversary. As soon as I think that he has resolved the impasse, I ask him how is the headache. Usually he no longer has it. If he is still holding on to it, we repeat the program. We never do this more than 5-6 minutes. If we are not successful, we quit and send the patient off to take some medication. If we continue to fail to resolve with a dialogue, we send the patient to a neurologist. We also teach migraine sufferers to do a short (up to five minutes) trial as soon as the aura starts; they often learn to abort the pain.

Sometimes we cannot get to a redecision. This is often true in suicidal or homicidal patients. When this occurs, we ask the patient for a contract not to kill the self or another accidentally or on purpose until the work is finished or until a specified future date. This has been a very effective method of keeping patients non-violent until they resolve the impasse. Depressed patients are very relieved when they no longer have daily fights against their suicidal impulse, are much more involved in the therapeutic process, and begin to claim their own autonomy. Of course, we must be sure that the work is finished by the future date or renew the date. For further examples of this or other impasse resolutions, see *Changing Lives* (Goulding & Goulding, 1979) or *Power is in the Patient* (Goulding & Goulding, 1978).

ANCHORING AND CHANGING STROKE PATTERNS

Anchoring is the process of supporting the patient's return to this victorious, autonomous moment, rather than responding to similar stress by the old, adaptive way. For instance, the next time Carol gets into an impasse with her supervisor, she will remember the current work and respond to him genuinely rather than by putting mother's face on him. The process of anchoring, then, changes the neurophysiologic pathways so that a confrontation with someone similar to the supervisor (and mother) does not automatically stimulate an angry response but rather the redecision response. Carol has thus closed the formerly open gestalt with a now-appropriate response; she has redecided not to adapt but to be Free and Adult in response to current stresses.

Working in groups, the applause and stroking after every impasse resolution does a lot towards anchoring. In addition, we build in other "fixing" processes. We ask the patient to imagine something she could call upon under stress. Carol referred to an imagined parrot in a cage with mother's face. Every time she began to react in the old way, she would imagine drawing a curtain over the parrot's cage! Several days later someone asked her to carry some chairs into the dining room. She looked baffled for a moment, then laughed, put her hands in the air, drew down the fantasy cage curtain, and walked off.

Other anchoring may include touching. We are very careful not to touch or allow touching when a patient is still in an old "racket" response. We do touch and encourage others in the group to touch in order to anchor when it comes naturally. We may ask the patient at the end of the work if she wants anything from anybody and let her ask for a hug, or someone may warmly volunteer. We might hug at the next break. Some therapists rush across the room, touch the patient and say, "Now anchor that." That seems too contrived to me. I prefer to touch in a more natural and spontaneous way.

PLAN FOR THE FUTURE

Before the work is finished, we ask people to plan how they are going to use their redecision in the future. Our work-hard patient planned to watch herself so she would not respond in the old way and to lay down some rules about overtime. She also decided to get her work in on time and when that was not possible, to talk to her supervisor rather than rebel. She also decided if it turned out that her supervisor was intractable, she would get another job — peacefully.

The kind of plans people make, of course, depend upon the situation. Carol made plans, after her Type 2 work, regarding her unwillingness to be childlike, to play with ideas, and to have fun. She started to say, "I'll work on that," but caught herself and laughed. She said, instead, "I'll play with that!" A real victory.

SUMMARY

Redecision Transactional Analysis is designed to help patients claim their autonomy. The work leads them to the maladaptive resolutions of impasses. Their task is to make new decisions about how they want to respond to old or familiar situations. The TA therapist's task is to facilitate their anchoring that redecision so that when under future stress, they will respond in the new non-adaptive way.

NOTES

1. This article makes the assumption that the reader knows some of the basic concepts of TA. For more information about classical Transactional Analysis, the games, and the Ego States, see Eric Berne (1961; 1964; 1977).

2. I have had conversations about this phenomenon with Ian Alger, John Gladfelter, and Milton Berger, therapists known for their use of video.

REFERENCES

Berne, E. (1961). *Transactional analysis in psychotherapy*. New York: Grove Press.

Berne, E. (1964). *Games people play*. New York: Grove Press.

Berne, E. (1977). *Intuitions and ego states: The origins of transactional analysis*. San Francisco: TA Press.

Goulding, M. (In press). *Not to worry*. New York: William Morrow/Silver Arrow.

Goulding, R., & Goulding, M. (1978). *The power is in the patient*. San Francisco: TA Press.

Goulding, R., & Goulding, M. (1979). *Changing lives*.

Chapter 6

Teaching Group Therapy
Within Social Work Education

Paul H. Ephross

INTRODUCTION

A discussion of educating students for the practice of group therapy within the broader framework of social work education poses
dangers for anyone who attempts to write it as well as for the
reader, for a number of reasons. Social work education is an enormous enterprise. It takes place in the context of a very wide gamut
of universities, both in this country and throughout the world. De-
spite efforts made in the United States and elsewhere to set standards by ways of accreditation requirements, the diversity in the
sponsoring institutions results, as it is bound to, in a diversity of
theoretical approaches, teaching methods and curriculum formats.

A second dilemma results from changes and evolutions in the
structure of social work education. After a period of controversy as
to whether social work curricula should exist at the graduate level
only, at both undergraduate and graduate levels, or exclusively at
the undergraduate level, the matter seemed to be resolved in favor
of the Master's degree during the 1950s and '60s, with only a few
programs continuing at the baccalaureate level. This consensus

Paul H. Ephross, PhD, is Professor, School of Social Work and Community
Planning, University of Maryland at Baltimore, 525 West Redwood Street, Baltimore, MD 21201.

87

turned out to be illusory. Beginning in the late 1960s and continuing to the present, there has been a proliferation of undergraduate programs. At the time of writing, there are several hundred "BSW" programs. Each needs to meet basic criteria if it is to be accredited by the Council on Social Work Education, the official accrediting body in the United States. It is probably fair to note, however, that the diversity among undergraduate programs is even greater than that which characterizes the graduate programs.

Yet another source of complexity comes from the changing structure of graduate social work education with regard to the ways in which the curriculum is organized. Changes and evolution continue from year to year, but some patterned regularities can be seen. At one time, the standard pattern was for graduate programs to be organized around, and to offer "concentrations" or "majors" in the various social work methods. These were defined as social casework (social work with individuals, sometimes with a nod in the direction of social work with families), social group work (of which more below), and community organization, which in the context of the times referred primarily to interagency and interorganizational work. Administration and, once in a while, research were also offered by a few schools. By now, though, this methodological principle of organization, though still in use in some schools, has been supplanted in others either by organization around social problems or particular populations — such as urban families, social work in health care, or social work with the aged — or by a grid or matrix approach which combines the two. Other programs have combined methods, so that areas of concentration seek to include more than one practice method. Clinical Social Work and Social Treatment are examples of attempts to teach both individual and group work skills on behalf of particular kinds of clients and client-systems. Not only group therapy or treatment, but all of social work with groups becomes merely one of several modes for working with social work clients.

Finally, it seems to this writer that group therapy or treatment has been viewed within social work education and within the social work profession as a subset of a broader method, process and field of practice called social group work, historically, but in recent years more often named social work with groups. After a period of decline into relative obscurity, group work is enjoying a noticeable and continuing revival within social work (Papell and Rothman, 1988). For the most part, however, though many schools offer advanced-level courses on group treatment or group therapy, the basic point of view remains one which identifies group therapy as one mode, or application, of a more generally defined group work method. Thus, it is difficult for anyone to discuss teaching group therapy to social work students and practitioners without a more general discussion of the processes of teaching and learning about group work in general.

The importance of this point has been reinforced for me by the experiences gained in the course of teaching and supervising psychiatric residents who are working with groups for therapeutic purposes. Understandably, their mental set is to view group therapy as a derivative, a subset, as it were, of individual therapy. Much useful learning engagement can take place around examining this set of intellectual and emotional assumptions. For most social work faculty and many experienced practitioners, on the other hand, group therapy is viewed as a particular kind of group work practice, akin to social work with educational-developmental groups, informal educational groups, work groups, and the like. I do not mean to imply that most social work students begin their social work education with the latter view. Quite to the contrary, because of the great prestige of the psychiatric model and because a fair proportion of social work students have experience as members of therapeutic groups, the word, "group" tends to summon an association of "therapy," an association which many social work teachers go to some lengths to reduce or at least bring under a more conscious control.

In summary, then, it is difficult to characterize any one approach as *the* social work education approach. What follows is a personalized account by one social work teacher who believes that his approach is not atypical of those used by many other teachers who view themselves as part of the mainstream of social work education.

INTELLECTUAL UNDERPINNINGS

To me, the line between group theory and group work practice has always been a thin one. For members of an action-oriented profession, to understand carries with it two obligations: to apply one's understandings in one's own conscious participation in groups, and to apply one's understandings in the professional role in groups, whether that role is called staff, worker or therapist. So, one needs to know about groups in order to be an effective group therapist. What does one need to know? Here is an incomplete list:

(1) One needs to know a typology, or nosology of types of collectivities, so that one understands the differences between mature small groups and collectivities that are not. It is especially important for group therapists to understand group-like phenomena that take place in quasi-groups. Sometimes, I like to call these quasi- or non-groups, "groupoids," just so that students will get the point.

(2) One needs to understand the place of group experiences in the development of the human personality and in the socialization and resocialization of people. In order to understand this place, one needs a well-developed theoretical framework about both the development of individual personality and about the social psychology of group life. Both an ego-psychological framework and a symbolic interactionist one suggest themselves as useful for these purposes. A group is, after all, largely a symbolic entity, and modern ego-psychological personality theories (e.g., object relations theory) are useful for understanding the place of group experiences in their members' lives.

(3) Stage or phase models of group development are rich with implications for the practitioner with groups. All of the various stage models or frameworks are useful, and their congruence with each other is very striking, giving promise as it does that we may be on the verge of truly synthesizing a theory of group life and group work. My own favorite for teaching, perhaps because it was originally drawn from the examination of practice and remains close to practice, is the five-stage model of group development which has become known in social work as the "Boston Model" (Garland, Jones, and Kolodny, 1965), now undergoing further testing and elaboration by Garland (1988).

(4) At least a beginning appreciation of the effects of group activities, including the relevant variables which can have an effect on group processes, is necessary. There is an unfortunate tendency for therapeutic groups to seek to confine their repertoire of activities to talking. The verbal medium is not necessarily the best one for dealing with strong feelings on the part of group members, for experiencing the kinds of closeness and warmth which therapy groups at their best are so good at generating, nor for enabling individual group members to take on different roles and use the group as a safe learning laboratory. Having noted this, one should take care to distinguish between helping students develop comfort with the kinds of activities which are useful in work with treatment groups and teaching actual skills at these activities. One is appropriate for teaching group therapy and the other is not; one need not try to teach students how to sing, or even how to lead singing, to help them understand that there may well be group situations, with certain kinds of memberships, in which singing is useful in order to help the group experience a particular mood or tone or express a particular shared yearning.

(5) It is helpful for social work students to know something of the history of work with groups, both within and outside of social work. Thus, Schwartz (1971, pp. 3-5) has pointed out that Mary Richmond in 1920, Edward Lindeman in 1939, the classical group work writers in the period from 1949 on, all pointed to the central position that work with groups should have within the range of social work practice.

(6) It is also helpful for students to learn that there are a variety of approaches to working with treatment groups, each of which has advantages and disadvantages, each of which may be more appropriate to one specific set of group purposes and group composition, and less so to another. In this way, students can be free from the constraints of what has elsewhere been termed "technology worship." Two examples of comparative approaches are given later in this discussion: co-therapy versus single therapy, and the question of guidelines for activity on the part of the therapist(s).

(7) Students need a conceptual framework for guiding their actual work in the role of therapist. Two approaches to this teaching and learning task are possible, at least. The first is to root the framework

specifically in the group therapeutic enterprise. Yalom's third edition of his celebrated text (1984) does a humanistic job of setting this forth. My own preference, however, is to take a conceptual framework for group treatment from a more general framework for work with groups. For this purpose, though supplementation by a teacher is needed, it is hard to fault Schwartz' little essay, "On the Use of Groups in Social Work Practice"(1971).

Noting that this list is a partial one, and that there is much more to be learned cognitively about groups and about group work which the developing group therapist will find useful, let us turn to look more specifically at the learning experiences which are designed to teach skills and an attitudinal set which is conducive to effective and skilled guidance of therapeutic groups.

GROUP EXERCISES AND ROLE PLAYS

Although there is a shortage of carefully produced records of treatment groups for teaching practice, and anyone who contributes to the limited supply deserves the thanks of the therapeutic professions, there is no shortage of actual and potentially adaptable group exercises. These can be drawn from a variety of sources and I use several. The first is collections of simulations, games and training exercises. Many of these are written as situation-specific, but they can easily be adapted to group treatment situations. The second source is made up of games and everyday activities, again useful with or without adaptations. The third consists of original productions, usually by the teacher, but sometimes done by students, in the form of role plays.

With the proper safeguards — an ability on anyone's part to withdraw and proper prohibitions against playing one's self — role plays provide a rich and rewarding learning opportunity. One of the most important variables in designing a role play is the extent to which it is to be scripted. Roles plays can vary from a very open-ended situation, described in a short paragraph, perhaps with individual roles noted below in a sentence each, to elaborately scripted plays, some of which demand considerable acting talent and are capable of great impact on their classroom audiences. Techniques such as guided imagery have emerged from earlier use of stories. Collective, spontaneous dramatic skits can be used to bring reality to a situation.

In an academic setting, I have serious question about requiring and giving academic credit for participation in experiential exercises. In a purely professional setting, whether it involves field internship, continuing education, training and development experiences for staff, or whatever, it is hard to find substitutes for the immediacy and ability to involve people in their own learning that well-designed and well-presented exercises can have. The closest that I have come to solving this dilemma is to offer students, each semester, an experiential evening which they are urged but not required to attend. The vast majority usually do participate, and the session provides us with an opportunity to experiment with leadership roles, with experiential approaches that are drawn from various sources and are appropriate for groups at various stages of development. It also generates some cohesive feelings which can serve as an antidote to the feelings of alienation—no stranger to graduate programs of professional education.

Whenever one uses experiential exercises, of course, one needs to keep several angles of vision open. The first involves the purpose for which the exercise is being used in the group, whether with students or with therapy group members. A second is on the variables available to the therapist in designing and presenting the exercise. How much sharing is called for by the design of the exercise and how much can be done by individuals on their own? How much control is necessitated by the structure of the individual roles in the exercise? What are the cultural and sub-cultural meanings of the activity and of the behaviors which the activity calls for? What is the operational definition of membership which is activated by the activity? Where does this particular exercise, structured and presented in the way that it is, put the therapist? In the role of observer? Participant? In control? Deliberately out of the controlling, "leader" position? Constrained by the limits of a particular role? Free to move around and participate consciously and therapeutically?

DEALING WITH STUDENT FEARS

Most students approach learning about work with groups in general, and doing group therapy in particular, with many well-defined fears and some vague ones. Some of these fears are to be expected, and are merely group analogues of the same kinds of fears experienced at the beginning of work with individuals. Often, these fears are phrased in the form, "How will I know when to . . .?" A supportive stance on the part of the teacher, some reassurance that these are natural, developmental feelings and, occasionally, a bit of humor generally helps with these jitters. Some other fears need exploration in the learning process, whether this is done in the classroom, the field instruction conference, group supervision, or wherever.

These fears arise within the students and are clearly transferential in nature. One approach to dealing with this fact is to ask students whether any of the phenomena they fear have ever happened to them or to other students they know about. With very, very few exceptions, the answers are always in the negative. Pointing this out does not make the fears any the less real, but it does constitute the first step towards helping students look at the sources of their fears and thus, usually, towards overcoming them.

The first is a fear of harm. Sometimes it is expressed as a fear of being harmed by the group; for example, a fear that the group will suddenly turn on the therapist in some destructive way, perhaps physically. Sometimes a similar fear is expressed in reverse as an overconcern that the student will do something wrong or make some mistake which will bring some sort of incalculable harm to the group's members. Most often, the fear of being overwhelmed and the fear of hurting the group can both be understood as a fear of losing control on the students' parts. As experienced group therapists know, groups are places of comparative safety, particularly once they have developed mature mechanisms and gyroscopic abilities to recenter themselves.

A second is a fear of not knowing what to do. This fear, in turn, stems from a mixed sense of omnipotence and impotence, or, perhaps better phrased, an ambivalence about responsibility and ability to respond appropriately to the group. What is missed by this ambivalence and clouded by fears and a sense of inadequacy is the nature of the actual professional role of the therapist. In many ways, the therapist is more comparable to an orchestra's conductor than to a principal oboist. The therapist's task is largely that of a process specialist, to energize the potential group and to help it "turn itself on" so that it may be the source of the kind of help which justifies its existence to start with.

Realizing this fact helps students free themselves from the over-powering anxiety which can accompany the ambivalence noted above. Reminding students that the reasons for treating people in groups center around the power of the group—*not the therapist, but the group*—to provide therapeutic experiences for its members re-lieves the therapist from the self-imposed responsibility of knowing all, being able to respond to everything, and knowing what to say at all times. Traditional ways of reminding students of this include discussion of "ownership" of the group and "ownership" of its problems. It is interesting and always rewarding for a teacher to note the growth that takes place as a class or an individual student comes to grips with the fact that they need not feel inadequate be-cause they are not filled with answers to all actual and potential group problems. Along with this realization comes an internalized understanding that group therapy is something quite different than the public treatment of individuals, and that a pattern of communi-cation which goes therapist—member A—therapist—member B—therapist—member C, and so on, is actually subversive of the for-mation of a genuine group as often as not.

Some other fears deserve mention, though the limitations of space prevent us from discussing them fully. One of them is the fear of intimacy which sometimes results in students' blocking, overtly or covertly, the group from dealing with highly charged material, particularly material of a sexual nature. Sometimes, the overt per-ception by students is that "the group isn't ready" when, in fact, it is the student-therapist who isn't ready. Working with groups for therapeutic purposes means that a therapist needs to maintain be-havioral and participation control at the same time that strongly charged group emotional climates stir feelings in the therapist as well as in the group members.[1]

Another fear often experienced by beginning group therapists has to do with differences of social class, educational level, race or ethnicity, age, or condition of handicap between themselves and group members. Each of these differences does constitute a potential barrier to effective communication between therapist and group members. Each, however, also constitutes an opportunity, once barriers have been overcome, for mutual enrichment of the group's processes and help to its members. My own approach to issues of differences is to assume that they constitute a barrier to some extent, given our society's discomforts with differences. If one makes this assumption and is "disappointed" to find that it is mistaken, so much the better. If, however, the differences need to be worked through, one is prepared for this process.

The last of the fears to be addressed here deserves special consideration: this is the fear of working with a group in a solo therapist position.

CO-THERAPY AND SOLO THERAPY

In some settings, it is assumed that co-therapy—two therapists per group—is a *desideratum*. Where this is based on a realistic assessment of the needs of a group and its members, the nature of the behavior to be expected from a particular group or a particular group's purpose, then co-therapy makes very good sense. Another reason for doing group therapy with a partner is the fact that one of the therapists is a trainee, either in working with groups in general or in working with a particular kind of group, utilizing a particular technique, or developing a particular format.

It is my position that in the absence of a particular reason for co-therapy, group therapy is best carried out by *a solo therapist*. There are several reasons for this. The first is that of cost. Two therapists per group is simply a very expensive situation, both in terms of money and in terms of available therapeutic resources. Second, the solo therapeutic situation is simpler; it provides fewer opportunities for complex game-playing between individual members and the group as a whole and the therapist. Third, communication is simpler. Fourth, therapists are free to utilize their own particular styles, express themselves in their own unique ways, etc.

The reader may object, and correctly, that there are several kinds of groups which seem to demand co-therapy. Groups formed around couples' problems are one example, though one should note that, depending on who comprises the couples, a straight-gay team may make more sense than a male-female duo. Groups in which there is an actual or potential problem of control may justify a situation in which one therapist is free to leave the group's room while the other carries on with the group meeting. Groups composed half of members of one background and half of another may derive real benefit from co-therapists. One argument which does *not*, in my view, justify assigning more than one therapist is the notion that one therapist may "miss" something. Doubtless she or he will. Just as doubtless, it is not the job of the group therapist to "catch" everything, but rather to help a group develop whose processes and way of being will help its members.

CONCLUSIONS

Perhaps the most important part of the training of group therapists within social work education is conveying the power, the importance and the integrity of a therapeutic group as a helping engine, as a source of help for its members. One can attempt to teach this in the classroom, both as a result of experiential exercises, role plays, and other attempts to simulate a real group, and through discussion of conceptual frameworks and other cognitively oriented learnings about groups and about their development. All of this is important, but in the last analysis likely to be fruitless unless it is permeated by a profound sense of appreciation for what groups can accomplish, once they have been helped to form and to move through the inevitable early crises.

Group therapy, and the broader field of group work of which it is a part, exemplifies the concept of the professional as a process expert. Rather than viewing the professional as a healer, as someone who owns secrets which he can convey to others, the group therapist is more accurately an enabler, an empowerer, at times a teacher, the person who turns on a very potent helping engine to be operated by the other group members. The group therapist needs to learn to influence the emotional climate of groups in the direction of safety and civility for group members. At the same time, the group therapist needs to develop a deeply felt sense of safety and comfort in helping groups deal with conflict and with issues which exist both within the group and between the group and the larger organization which sponsors it.

In short, teaching group therapy within social work education means helping people learn that healing comes from within the group, and that people carry with them great resources for growth and recovery. There is no easy way and no royal road to learning these facts, but there is nothing more rewarding for a teacher than knowing that students and supervisees have learned these lessons.

NOTE

1. The therapist, of course, is also a member of the group in a descriptive sense, albeit a member with a specialized role.

REFERENCES

Garland, J.E., Jones, H.E., & Kolodny, R.L. A model for stages of development in social work groups, in S. Bernstein, ed. *Explorations in Group Work*. Boston: Boston University, 1965.

Garland, J.E. Stages of group development reconsidered, Institute presented at the Tenth Annual Symposium on Social Work with Groups, Baltimore, MD, October, 1988.

Papell, C.P. & Rothman, B. Editorial, *Social Work with Groups*, 1988, *11*, 1/2, 1-8.

Schwartz, W. On the use of groups in social work practice, in Schwartz, W. & Zalba, S.R. *The Practice of Group Work*. New York: Columbia University Press, 1971.

Weiss, J.C. The D-R model of coleadership of groups, *Small Group Behavior*, 1988, *19*, 1, 117-125.

Yalom, I. *Theory and Practice of Group Psychotherapy*, 3rd ed. New York: Basic Books, 1984.

Chapter 7

Consultation in Group Therapy with Children and Adolescents

Judith Coché

Consultation in pediatric group therapy is a unique clinical entity with its own skills and evaluation techniques. This article discusses the nature of consultation, how to choose a clinical consultant, key variables in the consultation process, and the necessary knowledge base for the consultant. The importance of integrating the consultation process into the institutional setting is discussed, and suggestions to the clinician for this integration are offered.

THE NATURE OF CONSULTATION

To consult someone basically means to seek her opinion on a particular matter. There is no contract assuring that the opinion will be of value, nor that it will be operationalized. There is no guarantee that the consultant's opinion will be suitable to the context within which the problem occurs. Contemplating this state of affairs I am reminded of a recent trip to Arizona. On what I believed to be a casual "tourist" visit to an Indian tribe near Phoenix, I found myself an invited guest of the tribe who had learned of my consultation skills to groups. For two hours, and at no fee, the tribe leader extemporaneously consulted me on matters of greatest import: rela-

Judith Coché, PhD, is Assistant Clinical Professor of Psychology in Psychiatry at the University of Pennsylvania, and Clinical Consultant to the Hilltop Preparatory School (Villanova, Pennsylvania). Inquiries may be addressed to 2037 Delancey Place, Philadelphia, PA 19103.

99

tions between their tribe and the city of Phoenix, relations between their tribe and the Bureau of Indian Affairs, diagnostic subtleties between learning disabilities and emotional disturbance as it affects the latency-aged Indian child. My repeated protests that I was not an expert at these matters made little difference and, most likely, the content of my consultation also made little difference in the handling of the problems. I was indeed, consulted, but to what end and with what value I may never know.

This experience acts as a contrast to the even more recent experience in helping a child guidance clinic launch a training program in Group Psychotherapy. Here, my skills were known in advance, and the terms of the contract spelled out before the program began. Numerous "briefings" about the nature of the institution and the trainees (staff and psychiatric fellows) were held with the senior staff. Weekly telephone contacts and meetings served to integrate the outside trainer with the shifting needs of the trainees as the initial course took form. Ongoing processing of course content and teaching materials, as well as post-course evaluations, rounded out my experience of beginning as a consultant in an unknown land — where I was figuratively a tourist, and I was asked not only to stay for dinner but to share in the family meetings as well. However, here the institution's utilization of the trainer's input became increasingly evident as the feedback loop circled round over the weeks. (See Diagram 1.)

The contrast between these two recent uses of my consultation skills provides an introduction in considering the issues central to doing or receiving professional consultation in group therapy with children and adolescents. Consulting with therapists doing group

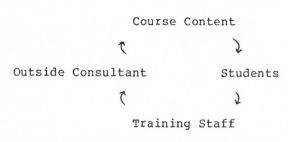

DIAGRAM 1. The Consultation Feedback Loop

psychotherapy is a tricky business if one does not enjoy feeling like the obligatory aunt who came to tea and stayed too long for the likes of everyone.

CHOOSING A CONSULTANT

Kaslow (1986), in discussing issues in choosing a supervisor or consultant, refers to the "vicarious liability" in supervision, but reiterates the "take it or leave it" quality of the consultation contract (p. 149). The consultant should be well respected, emotionally sound, competent, and an experienced clinician and supervisor.

For this author, four issues for selecting a group therapy consultant seem overriding:

1. *Content expertise*: The consultant is expected to have more knowledge of the content area than the consultees. It is crucial, for example, that a consultant of adolescent group psychotherapy have a working theory of adolescent development, have a command of cognitive development in adolescence, and have a firsthand knowledge of group work with this age.

2. *Stature among colleagues*: Most consultants are chosen because of an earned, or at least perceived, stature in their field. The "halo effect" afforded by such social perception functions to increase readiness on the part of colleagues to attend to the training offered.

3. *Ethical and moral conduct*: Recent attention has been focused on supervisors, trainers, and consultants entering into unethical professional contracts with trainees. I personally have supervised numerous female trainees with complaints such as flirtation and sexual innuendos from male supervisors, unequal career rights, and unequal respect in relation to male colleagues. This unfortunate reality makes it even more imperative for consultants who train professionals dealing with the social interaction of youngsters (for this *is* the nature of group therapy) to fulfill the expectation of an outstanding record in ethical conduct. If we are to act as models in professional development, it is imperative that we impart clear role boundaries and respect to the clinicians who in return model these traits for the children in our groups.

4. *Supervisory skill*: Numerous authors have addressed the quali-

ties involved in skillful supervision. The interested reader might pay special attention to work by Alonso (1985); Coché (1977); Coché (1984); Coché and Fisher (in press); Pinney (1983); Rutan and Stone (1984); and Soo (1986).

Supervisory skill is a preparation and necessary underpinning for good consultation. In fact, the consultant acts as a resource for the supervisory staff. Unlike the old adage, "Those who can't do, teach; those who can't teach, teach teachers," skillful consultation requires skill both in doing and in teaching.

KEY VARIABLES IN THE CONSULTATION PROCESS

Like consultation and training with professionals running adult groups, consultation with children's groups is best served by a regularity of structure and by some form of evaluation.

Structure of Consultation. Soo (1986) discusses the value of predictability in the time and in the location of training. The expectation that consultation will happen regularly, on time, and with the same people, provides the consistent external structure for self-disclosure that is so crucial in group therapy. This consistency adds credence to the value of the consultation. What happens within the solid external structure, of course, can vary. People feel safer to experiment and to take risks when they know the outer boundaries and know they are solid.

Student Evaluation. Occasionally the consultant will be asked to write or present an evaluation of the trainee's work. It is essential that such evaluations be honest even if this involves a certain degree of "toughness." Good work is easy to evaluate; it is unpleasant, though, to participate in an evaluation of work that is substandard. However, it is far more unthinkable to bypass, in the name of politeness, issues involving countertransference, unethical conduct, or other causes for concern. The key in such professional evaluations is one of mutual interpersonal respect: as long as the trainer maintains her own integrity and the integrity of the student, this attitude of mutual respect can be conveyed in even the most delicate of evaluative situations.

One of the more difficult tasks in evaluations is telling students they are not well suited to do child group therapy. Unless a trainee has extensive knowledge in academic child development, the trainee must be willing to learn about the group members from a developmental perspective. The incorporation of developmental milestones, central tasks, typical ethical dilemmas, etc., into treatment interventions for a group of any age insures the appropriateness of the therapeutic goals for that age group. Students who are impatient at the wealth of details necessary to learn about children would be better working with adults where the developmental phases are stable for longer time periods, or reconsidering if therapy is their best choice of a profession.

Bill was a graduate student in a university clinical training program. I had been asked to consult on his adolescent therapy group. Bill was bright, knowledgeable in group theory and research, facile and charming in his clinical interactions with groups. However, he had interpersonal conflicts with his fellow students who saw him as condescending. The teaching faculty noted that Bill was hard to train, primarily because he had a "slickness" which was hard to pin down. I decided to let the process unfold. About three months after the consultation began, Bill reported that he planned to see in his private practice, a child from one of his groups at the agency where he was in training. Since he was unlicensed, a "psychiatrist friend" would be signing to enable insurance reimbursements. The multiple conflicts of interest were obvious. First, there was no agency precedent for seeing clients privately and at the agency. Second, in legally endorsing an unlicensed trainee, the psychiatrist was in danger of professional backlash by signing for Bill without supervising him. Finally, Pennsylvania psychology licensing laws state that an unlicensed psychologist must be salaried by the supervising psychologist, who must be on site during service delivery. Bill was presented with the illegalities of his plan. Initially he was argumentative and tried cajoling the consultant. However, when the consultant held fast and warned him he would have to leave the training program if he persisted, he relented. After this incident, Bill became more cooperative, less manipulative, and used the consultation better.

DEVELOPMENTAL THEORIES FOR CHILD
AND ADOLESCENT GROUP THERAPY

Having outlined a handful of basic concepts in group consultation for all ages, I will now describe two key dimensions in pediatric group work supervision and consultation: knowledge of child developmental theory and stages of child development.

Theories of Child Development Theory

In order to establish a children's group and develop a solid treatment plan, it is essential that leaders work from a theoretical perspective that is both normative and developmental, and that they be knowledgeable about pathological childhood developments. Simply stated, it is difficult to discern what is pathological if one is unaccustomed to routine behavior at a given developmental level. Therefore, the consultant must be sure the child group therapists are aware of the major developmental theories and aware of normal and pathological behavior. (It is beyond the scope of this paper to address the full range of child behavior.)

Three of the most frequently used developmental theories are social learning, psychodynamic, and family systems. As discussed by Coché and Fisher (in press), understanding these theories will help the group therapist choose what type of group is best suited for which child and what type of interventions to make.

1. *Social learning theory.* A child or adolescent group can function as a human relations laboratory, in which skills, poorly learned at home or in school, can be reshaped into more appropriate and effective habits. Activity groups, social skill groups, assertiveness groups—all assume that social retraining is both necessary and possible for the members over a relatively short time. For example, a "rap" group for children whose parents are divorcing functions to undo misconceptions about the child's role in the divorce, and to educate members about the realities of living in a family where a divorce has occurred.

2. *Psychoanalytic theory.* For some children, a developmental block occurs when they have interpsychic or early interpersonal problems. The work of psychotherapy is assumed to be more inner-

directed, that is, between the young person and an introject of one or more family members, especially parents. In psychoanalytic child group therapy, techniques are therefore aimed at recreating, through discussion or through play, the conflicted material and reworking the material in the group.

3. *Family systems theory.* Family systems theory has recently attained considerable prominence because of its respect for the complexity of contextual change. The theory assumes that the function of therapy is to unravel current interfamilial behavioral patterns that interfere with a child's development. Unlike social learning theory, simple stimulus-response thinking is replaced by family concepts of triangulation and family homeostasis. Unlike psychoanalytic thinking, change does not occur through understanding and reexperiencing alone. Children seen in family therapy have the opportunity to clarify hierarchal roles, boundaries, alliances, etc., which frees them for healthier relationships among their peers.

It is imperative that the consultant exemplify clarity in theoretical and developmental thinking in order to help the group therapist adopt one theory or a blend of several theories as a basis for the children's group.

Stages of Child Development

A consultant needs to be thoroughly familiar not only with the basic theories of development but also with the stages of child development. The consultant must have a working knowledge of the physical as well as cognitive changes that occur within each stage. Twelve-year-old boys will be affected by their hormonal changes in ways that six-year-old girls are not. Preparation for groups and treatment plans should take these differences into account. The consultant needs to make sure that the child group therapist knows this information and takes it into consideration in planning for a group. In other words, a treatment plan for a group of children is only as good as the therapist's knowledge of what children at that age look like, act like, think about, and feel.

CREATING AN INSTITUTIONAL "FIT"

The skills of the consultant are only as valuable as her ability to enable her to work in the varying atmospheres of different institutions. Alonso (1985) describes the supervisor as serving the needs of the administration, the therapist, and the patient. In like fashion, the very skills in group process and systems analysis which ensure success in group treatment are equally applicable to the process between the trainer, the trainees, and the context of the institution. To illustrate these processes, we might think of concentric circles.

These expanding circles represent the overlapping influence each has on the other. Running a group without taking all of these levels into consideration leaves one open for difficulty at any point of contact. The consultant must keep clear boundaries with each hierarchical level and make sure the child group therapist does the same. Often difficulties in the group among members or between a member and the leader are a reflection of difficulties between two of the other concentric circles.

THE INSIDE-OUTSIDE NATURE
OF CONSULTATION

The outstanding consultant thrives on being peripheral. Like Yoda in the *Star Wars* trilogy, the consultant has a life clearly apart from the job at hand, yet has the capacity to join and distance from the inner workings of a staff. Key issues in a successful consultant experience, then, involve joining the staff and readying the staff for the consultation experience.

Joining with the Insiders

The consultant is an outsider attempting to join with the inside staff. In making that move, the consultant will experience several possible reactions from the staff. One reaction is that the staff feels simultaneously enthusiastic and distrustful of this new person. Much like a wizard, the consultant may be imparted with exaggerations in her capacity to do wonders. When she does not perform the miracles, the staff will feel cheated. Earning trust is a slow and arduous task. While the staff may initially ascribe status, wisdom, and acuity to the consultant, genuine acceptance comes later as the staff feels more relaxed and feels empowered by the consultant.

I was recently invited to pioneer formal training in group therapy to staff members and trainees at a prestigious child guidance clinic. There had been resistance to an earlier attempt to do this. Most of the participants were new to group therapy and believed the concepts were too complex and time consuming. In order to facilitate my joining, I stressed certain facets of the experience. First, I discussed openly my inside-outside status. I described my clinical life outside of this consultation. I related vignettes from my private practice groups to differentiate myself from the staff. I directly told the staff that I did not expect their trust; I was a stranger to them and I had not yet earned it. I encouraged staff participating in teaching activities and invited them to bring tapes of ongoing group therapy sessions to our seminar. In this way I simultaneously stressed my peripheral involvement and the power of my capacity to assist. Within the 20-week consultation, the staff and I moved from an initial "I/they" to a temporary "we" position—a sign of a successful consultation.

How do you create the "we"? How do you diminish the natural suspiciousness about an outsider? While there are many steps along the way, the most important one starts with recognizing that staff and trainees are key to an institution's progress and deserve recognition. Another major one reminds the consultant to be approachable and human, otherwise, she will be labelled esoteric or pedantic. Staff learn to keep distant from a consultant who has a greater need to be important than to be skillful.

In order to maximize the power of consultation activities, a consultant needs to maximize the readiness of the staff to participate in the ongoing consultation experience.

Readiness and Enthusiasm for Learning

Training opportunities in group therapy are too often introduced when the administration is ready to teach rather than when the trainees are ready to learn. The consequence is that trainees may want to be polite, but may actually be annoyed that they are being forced to learn group therapy with children. Internal resistances, such as shyness in groups, embarrassment at one's ignorance, discomfort with process material, act as obstacles to benefitting from, and enjoying being trained (Soo, 1986). On the other hand, other staff may welcome the consultant like an oasis in a perceived desert. The consultant needs to assess the involvement level of each staff member, working differently with those who are eager for training than with those who are there because they have to be.

Differences in readiness are easily apparent. Classic signs include lateness, stony silence, and absences. In one training experience, graduate students ranged from highly disinterested to highly interested. One student, forced to come to the training in order to meet his requirements, indicated his obvious discomfort and distaste by positioning his chair snugly in a far corner of the class, in back of the instructor's line of vision. Other class members, quite enthusiastic about the course sat in an inner circle around the table in the middle of the room. While the "corner" student remained silent week after week, with only occasional "grumbles" of disagreement, the students around the table demonstrated enthusiasm consistent with their central seating. They exhibited a willingness to read material and discuss it, to form a mock therapy group, and to participate in role playing.

A consultant needs to know when it is helpful to draw in a reluctant trainee and when it will be disruptive to the class. Clear lines of hierarchical authority (as demonstrated by the concentric circles) helps the consultant make this distinction.

CONCLUSION

In four major works (Kaslow, 1986; Kaslow et al., 1977; Hess, 1980; Riester & Kraft, 1986), fewer than twenty five pages are devoted to consultation in group therapy and nothing is mentioned about consultation in child and adolescent group therapy. In a brief review of the literature, I was struck with the paucity of information on consultation and supervision in group therapy with children and adolescents.

Since the invention of the written word and the teaching of written language, documentation and replication of the spoken word (legend, myth, and tradition) have been a hallmark which distinguishes professional endeavors from family folklore or amateur efforts. It is essential for professionals involved in the consultation process in group therapy with young people to document their knowledge and skills via the written word. It is only then that variables in the process can be isolated clearly enough to generate the type of research which is now common on the group psychotherapy process itself (Coché and Dies, 1981). The issues in this article provide a beginning in this direction.

REFERENCES

Alonso, A. (1985). *The quiet profession.* New York: Macmillan.
Coché, E. (1977). Training of group therapists. In Florence W. Kaslow & Associates, *Supervision, consultation, and staff training in the helping professions.* Washington: Jossey-Bass, pp. 235-253.
Coché, E., & Dies, R.R. (1981). Integrating research findings into the practice of group psychotherapy. *Psychotherapy: Theory, Research, and Practice, 18,* 4, pp. 410-416.
Coché, J. (1984). Psychotherapy with women therapists. In F. Kaslow (Ed.), *Psychotherapy with psychotherapists.* New York: The Haworth Press, Inc., pp. 151-169.
Coché, J., & Fisher, J. (In press). Group psychotherapy with learning disabled adolescents: The Hill Top model. In Azima, F. (Ed.), *Group psychotherapy with children and adolescents.* American Group Psychotherapy Association, Monograph III. New York: International Universities Press.
Hess, A. (Ed.) (1980). *Psychotherapy supervision.* New York: John Wiley & Sons.
Kaslow, F. (1986). Seeking and providing supervision in private practice. In F. Kaslow (Ed.), *Supervision and training: Models, dilemmas, and challenges.* New York: The Haworth Press, Inc., pp. 143-158.
Kaslow, F., & Associates. (1977). *Supervision, consultation, and staff training in the helping professions.* Washington: Jossey-Bass.
Pinney, E.L., Jr. (1983). Ethical and legal issues in group psychotherapy. In. H. Kaplan & B. Sadock (Eds.), *Comprehensive group psychotherapy* (2nd ed.). Baltimore: Williams & Wilkins, pp. 301-304.
Riester, A.E., & Kraft, I.A., (Eds.) (1986). *Child group psychotherapy.* Madison, CT: International Universities Press.
Rutan, S., & Stone, W. (1984). *Psychodynamic group psychotherapy.* Lexington, MA: Colamore Press.
Soo, E. (1986). Training and supervision in child and adolescent group psychotherapy. In A.E. Riester & I.A. Kraft (Eds.), *Child group psychotherapy.* Madison, CT: International Universities Press, pp. 157-171.

Chapter 8

Training Mental Health Clinicians to Lead Short-Term Psychotherapy Groups in an HMO

Barbara Sabin Daley
Gerri Koppenaal

Since its inception 18 years ago, the Harvard Community Health Plan (HCHP) has provided a health care alternative to traditional health care delivery systems. It was developed as an illness prevention model as opposed to the more familiar episodic treatment model in which patients' treatment was covered by insurance only when they presented with an established illness. Health maintenance organizations (HMO) are prepaid health insurance plans that emphasize preventive treatment and integration of clinical services. The incentive of the HMO is to prevent major illness by providing coverage of regular routine physical examinations. They are thus able to contain medical costs as the bulk of treatment is absorbed in the outpatient setting, not in the more costly inpatient hospitalization (Koppenaal & Ellis, 1986). It is this cost containment that allows the HMO to deliver a comprehensive service package to its members.

Since 1973, HMOs have been federally required to provide comprehensive mental health treatment to their members. This means

Barbara Sabin Daley, MSN, was formerly at the Harvard Community Health Plan as a researcher and clinician. Inquiries may be addressed to 9 Crofton Road, Waban, MA 02168.

Gerri Koppenaal, RN, MS, CS, is Coordinator of Group Psychotherapy Program at HCHP Cambridge Center, and is in private practice in Cambridge, MA.

111

that mental health clinicians must deliver inpatient, outpatient, and 24-hour emergency services. Specifically, psychiatric consultation and referral, crisis intervention, short-term treatment, and treatment for alcohol and drug abuse must be included in the mental health benefit (Koppenaal & Ellis, 1986).

State laws regulate HMO services as well. In Massachusetts, HMOs must cover up to $500 of necessary outpatient treatment annually. They also must cover up to 60 days of inpatient hospitalization, 120 days of partial hospitalization or day treatment and 30 days of inpatient, alcohol and drug treatment (Koppenaal & Ellis, 1986).

Currently, HCHP delivers treatment to 200,000 members in nine centers in and around the Boston area. Approximately, 10% of these members utilize mental health services annually. It remains a challenge to provide a meaningful and useful treatment experience to all who seek mental health services. The decision was made in the inception of HCHP to limit not the availability of services, but the duration of services. Therefore, HCHP now offers a wide variety of brief treatment opportunities to its members.

Over the years, clinicians have come to regard brief-term psychotherapy not just as shortened long-term treatment or the poor relative to "real" (long-term) psychotherapy. Brief therapy now exists as a separate and valuable modality with distinct characteristics. The authors have found that this model of therapy successfully addresses many of the treatment needs presented by members of HCHP.

Budman and Gurman (1988) outline some pertinent differences in the treatment values of the short-term and long-term therapist. First, they suggest that a long-term therapist seeks to change a patient's basic character in therapy whereas the short-term therapist values "pragmatism, parsimony and the least radical intervention." The short-term therapist does not seek a "cure" (Budman & Gurman, 1988).

Secondly, they suggest that a long-term therapist does not believe that significant psychological change will occur normally. The short-term therapist, conversely, embraces an adult developmental model in which substantial psychological evolution is considered inevitable. Thirdly, where the long-term therapist views symptoms as indicators of more profound pathology, the short-term therapist capitalizes upon patients' strengths and resources. In this model, presenting problems are seriously addressed (Budman & Gurman, 1988).

While the long-term therapist wants to witness significant changes in patients, the short-term therapist realizes that many changes will occur after treatment has terminated and will not be observed by the therapist. Budman and Gurman (1988) further propose that the long-term therapist sees therapy as being open-ended and is willing to wait for change whereas the short-term therapist does not accept the "timelessness" of some treatment models. Additionally, the long-term therapist consciously or unconsciously is aware of the fiscal advantages of keeping patients in treatment whereas fiscal issues are often legislated by the organizational structure for reimbursement in a short-term model (Budman & Gurman, 1988).

They further suggest that the long-term therapist almost always views psychotherapy as being useful whereas the short-term therapist considers that while psychotherapy can be at times useful, it can be harmful as well.

Finally, Budman and Gurman (1988) submit that a long-term therapist sees patients being in therapy as the focal point of their life whereas a short-term therapist views "being in the world as more important than being in therapy."

Over time, clinicians at HCHP, though they recognize the value of long-term treatment for some patients, have largely adapted the short-term therapeutic values outlined by Budman and Gurman. These values, which subscribe to an interpersonal, developmental, and existential approach to therapy, apply to the practice of short-term psychotherapy in groups.

Given the mandate to see many patients while containing costs, it is not surprising that an extensive group psychotherapy program evolved at HCHP. Initially, HCHP therapists regarded groups as eight individual therapies occurring at once, or as a somewhat unsavory alternative to individual treatment if one's practice happened to be full. However, as with the brief-term individual program, necessity was the mother of invention. Over time, clinicians began to establish a theoretical model for doing short-term group psychotherapy. In fact, therapists could refer patients to a group as the treatment of choice without guilt about providing second-rate treatment. A shift in emphasis took place. The group as opposed to the therapist became viewed as the therapeutic agent. Though the therapist certainly played a role as a facilitator of process, it was the patient's experience with the group itself that provided the opportunity for self-exploration and eventual change.

Currently, therapists view group therapy as an opportunity rather than as a liability. There are approximately 24 groups running at any given time at one center alone. The groups are based on a developmental model for treatment. Therefore, patients who are in similar developmental phases in their lives are likely to be referred to the same kind of group. For example, if a 25-30 year-old man has experienced difficulty forming an intimate relationship, he might be referred to a coed young adult group. There, he might explore the parameters of significant relationships in his life in an effort to understand his current pain. The patient would be likely to examine relationships with his family. However, the relationships formed or not formed in the group would also provide a rich resource for understanding his feelings in relationships outside the group. The opportunity for change therefore exists within the context of the group process.

A woman in her thirties who is having difficulties caring for herself within the context of relationships, deferring to others' needs above her own may well be referred to a women's group. In this situation, she might be able to explore her need to accommodate others in relationships and her fear of losing a loved one should she express needs and demands of her own. Again, her therapeutic experience includes not only an examination of relationships in her life outside of the group, but of those within the context of the group as well. She might defer to other group members, be supportive and encourage them to talk. While she behaves this way, she may be silently furious about the fact that her needs are not being met. The process in the group mimics the process in her life. She has an opportunity to explore this pattern as it is happening in the group and thus to apply this learning to her life at large.

Patients who are referred for short-term group psychotherapy are generally free of major mental illness. They are able to tolerate their own affect as well as the affect of other group members. They are not dependent upon substances, and they must be developmentally appropriate for the group to which they are referred (Budman & Gurman, 1988). In brief-term, individual psychotherapy, it is essential to establish a focus at the outset of treatment. The therapist must likewise establish a focus for the group before the group begins (Budman & Gurman, 1988). For example, a young adult group's focus may be the establishment of intimate relationships. In addition, individual members set their own personal goals before the group begins.

STAGES OF GROUP DEVELOPMENT

Though different issues peculiar to specific developmental stages are addressed in different groups, we have found that short-term developmental groups follow a similar pattern regardless of focus. The group process can be divided into four stages: the initial stage, group crisis, the working stage, and termination.

First Stage

In the initial stage of a 15-session group (approximately sessions one through four), patients are beginning to get to know one another. They establish their similarities on a superficial level, and feel gratified by the fact that someone shares their life view and some of their pain. A sense of cohesion begins to form in the group. Budman (1987) suggests that cohesion is to group psychotherapy what the therapeutic alliance is to individual treatment. They describe cohesiveness as a multifaceted concept characterized by the following parts:

1. Withdrawal and self-absorption versus interest and involvement
2. Mistrust versus trust
3. Disruption versus cooperation
4. Abusiveness verses expressed caring
5. Lack of focus versus focus

During this stage, therapists should encourage the development of cohesion by encouraging interaction between members rather than between themselves and an individual member. They should also miss no opportunity to use the group experience as a forum for learning rather than relying solely upon the reporting of external events.

Second Stage

In the beginning stage, there is a sense of timelessness. The existential limitation of time has not yet emerged as an issue.

By the second or crisis stage of the group (sessions five through eight), patients begin to feel the need for "something more." The superficial aspect of the first stage is beginning to cloy. They begin to feel dissatisfied, disappointed or angry that the group is not doing more for them. At this stage in the group, cohesiveness decreases. Group members withdraw, becoming angry and defensive in response to their feelings of disappointment. They begin to realize that time in the group is limited. They yearn for more depth and resolution to their pain. They feel disappointed and angry that the therapist and the group have not actively resolved their focal problem. Time is half over. They are frustrated and frightened by this limitation. It is not unusual at this stage for members to become bored or withdrawn from the group. Some patients may voice their angry feelings openly while others talk about other disappointing authority figures or situations in their lives.

It is important at this point for therapists not to be intimidated by the group's anger. They should address the direct or indirect disappointment. Existential limitations of time are a real part of life as is the limited capacity of any individual or group to accommodate one's needs. This disappointment and sense of loss must be dealt with in the group so that group members may reestablish their sense of cohesiveness and move on to the third stage — the working stage.

Third Stage

In this stage of the group (sessions nine through thirteen), members have begun to deal with the existential feelings of loss and disappointment that emerged in the second phase. A subtle shift has taken place. Members now depend more on themselves to address focal conflicts. The group leader is now less of an authority figure, or idealized bearer of all things good, and more of a collaborator and facilitator. The cohesiveness of the group increases as members tackle their difficulties in more depth and are able to more openly trust each other. In this stage, it is important for therapists to address the process of the group. They must then help make that process relevant to the members' lives outside of the group.

Final Stage

The final stage of the group (sessions fourteen and fifteen) is termination. Members make peace with their strengths and limitations as well as the strengths and limitations of other significant people in their lives inside and outside of the group.

The overall experience of these groups is intense. Therapists are called upon to be active, yet not controlling. They must be very involved in a facilitating, yet not a pedantic way. They must be vigilant about the subtleties of group process—relating not only to the group but to life outside the group. Finally, they must be able to communicate this connection thus enhancing the process, not stifling it.

TRAINING

Many therapists at HCHP run short-term groups. Not all of them view the experience as a fascinating opportunity. We were somewhat puzzled as to what were the group training needs. We submitted a questionnaire to all HCHP clinicians. What follows is a description of the questionnaire and of a training program we are in the process of creating.

Training Survey

It has been documented that one should complete a thorough assessment of students' needs for learning before establishing a teaching program. Although we assumed no formal group therapy training was occurring regularly at HCHP, we were not sure whether senior staff members in the newer HCHP centers were providing consultation for new clinicians or promoting outside training in this area. We decided to send a survey to all mental health staff members at each of the nine clinical centers. We wished to evaluate each clinician's past and present experiences in group psychotherapy as well as their training requirements in this area. We encouraged participants to elaborate on their concerns at the end of a multiple choice questionnaire. We sent out 100 questionnaires and received back 70 which were answered completely. Staff members from the newer centers produced an 80% return while staff members from the older centers returned 50% of their questionnaires. This suggested to us either that new staff members were more motivated for training or that senior staff members were preoccupied with other priorities.

We asked participating clinicians to answer eleven questions. We first inquired about staff members' group therapy experience prior to coming to HCHP. Since the work expectation of all new staff is that they be experienced to lead groups autonomously from the date of hire, we expected positive answers to this question. We were surprised to find that therapists had equal experience leading short-term and long-term groups before coming to the HCHP. Only five therapists had not led a group. Several years ago few staff members entered HCHP with no short-term group experience. We did not ask clinicians to describe their groups. In particular, they did not note whether the groups were in inpatient or outpatient settings.

We were concerned about each clinician's current short-term group therapy commitment. We found that more staff members were leading short-term than long-term groups on a two-to-one ratio. All staff members led at least two groups annually and, for many, the primary treatment modality was either short- or long-term groups. Psychiatrists led more long-term groups while social workers and psychiatric nurse clinical specialists led more short-term groups. Only two staff members led groups reluctantly. The older centers had more staff members and larger group programs.

We inquired about each staff member's prior and current training in short-term group psychotherapy and whether they desired more training. Most staff members reported that they had taken a group psychotherapy course in graduate school or had had group therapy supervision. Approximately a third of the respondents had participated in an ongoing psychotherapy seminar or T-group training. All staff members had group psychotherapy training prior to their employment at HCHP. Their current group psychotherapy training was limited. The older centers offered organized weekly peer group supervision which not all staff members could attend due to time constraints. Many had co-led an HCHP group with a more senior HCHP therapist. Some used either their team meetings to present a group problem or caught colleagues informally in the hallway for impromptu supervision. The predominant message was that there was no structured training. More than two-thirds of the staff members (56 to 14) wanted more group psychotherapy training if they could work out the logistics of time and cross-center transportation. Most respondents favored creating a group psychotherapy seminar while a third wanted more weekly peer supervision. A few respondents wanted individual supervision with a senior staff person.

We also questioned staff members about what areas of short-term group psychotherapy they found most difficult and, therefore, what topics they would like to have included in a group psychotherapy seminar. Staff members found starting a group most difficult. The child psychotherapy clinicians had particular difficulty finding eight children at the same developmental level to start together. Screening and time limitations also presented problems to respondents. Clinicians were also concerned about effectively addressing different forms of group resistance, most particularly silence. Other concerns included termination, transference, and establishment of an early focus for treatment. Respondents were confused about the effectiveness of individual versus group interventions in a therapy group. Many respondents wished to learn how to plan groups with specific patient populations in different settings. Lastly, they wished to combine didactic material and experiential learning using student presentations of videotaped group meetings in a group psychotherapy seminar.

We asked staff members whether they thought that short-term and long-term groups were helpful to patients. Their choices were either or both. To our amazement, all respondents thought both short-term and long-term group therapy was helpful, depending on clinical facts of a case and the client's preferences.

In summary, we learned a great deal about staff members' specific needs and wishes for a group psychotherapy training program. Staff members were eager for cross-center exposure to group therapy problems and exposure to techniques for solving those problems.

Some staff members offered to help us design group training for specific populations; i.e., substance abusers, clients with eating disorders, incest survivors, children of divorced parents, or adult children of alcoholics. They were concerned about time and cost pressure to refer clients to groups when, even though it was clinically appropriate, the member did not prefer group treatment.

A few staff members recommended two separate training programs. The first would be a basic seminar to teach clinicians with little prior group training the basis of group dynamics and treatment. This would be taught by senior staff members. A more advanced course that was peer based would provide staff members with a forum to share useful treatment techniques and strategies and to expand their treatment horizons.

Outline for the Future Training Program

Plans for a formal, 15-week centralized short-term group psychotherapy training seminar are now in progress. This program will meet at one location and be open to staff members from different centers. Faculty will present didactic material and videotapes of groups. Students will present their own cases and video illustrations.

We believe that short-term group psychotherapy training is best done with a short-term group training course. Our hypothesis which we will share is that participants in the seminar will experience a process that mirrors the clients' experience in short-term group psychotherapy. Education is usually more effective for students when the training setting approximates as closely as possible the setting being discussed. Some processes that will be mirrored are: early group awkwardness and the gradual development of cohesion; possible wavering of enthusiasm and questioning of the value of the experience about five sessions into the process; problems with time limitations; and certain members' problems and termination. We do not believe that education and psychotherapy are the same or that one training seminar should merge the two. We do not plan to make the group seminar an experimental group therapy for staff members. We are simply expecting that the development of the trainee's group and the difficulties it faces may help the trainee understand a client's experience. The vulnerability that therapists encounter during videotape disclosure of their short-term groups will mirror the vulnerability clients often face during self-disclosure. These situations could be thought of as a group educational transference. What happens in certain developmental sessions of the seminar will relate very closely to what will occur at a similar time in the group psychotherapy.

Outline of a Short-Term Group Psychotherapy Training Seminar

Below is our basic sketch of the seminar: Trainees will be asked to videotape all fifteen weeks of one of their groups before the training seminar begins. They will show five to ten minute segments of this videotape series at different times in the course; i.e., at the beginning of the seminar, beginning group tapes will be shown. The seminar will run for fifteen weeks for one and one-half hours weekly, the same as a fifteen-week group psychotherapy. After the course, trainees will videotape another fifteen session group, which they may examine on their own or with one of the seminar leaders. Before the beginning of the seminar, trainees will be sent some didactic material on short-term group psychotherapy and on group cohesion. They will sign up to present two or three five- to ten-minute video segments of a developmental stage of their group which illustrates either problematic group process or therapist intervention. They might also show a segment which demonstrates a particularly effective intervention.

The mirroring of seminar process with short-term group psychotherapy will start in the first session with a discussion of personal objectives for the fifteen weeks. After going over logistics and ground rules for the seminar, group leaders will stimulate discussion by presenting minicase examples that address a new staff member's anxiety about doing time-limited group therapy. An example of a minicase is as follows: One meets a colleague at a party who learns that you have both participated in long-term group therapy. The colleague asks, "How can you possibly expect your clients to get anything out of fifteen group therapy sessions?'' How do you respond? Presentation of minicases like this will stimulate a discussion of the values and theoretical premises that relate to short-term developmental group psychotherapy in contrast to other theoretical group therapy modes.

We will then discuss screening and preparation for groups. At HCHP, we have developed a pre-group therapy screening workshop (Budman & Gurman, 1988). This is a pre-group seminar in which prospective group clients meet other people who may be in their group. The clients and therapist can assess whether they can utilize a group setting. A set of exercises is structured in this one screening session to observe individual and group behavior and to prepare the clients for how they can utilize the group in the future. Our plan for the training seminar is to mimic the pre-group workshop with the trainees using problem sharing exercises and role playing that addresses screening problems. A large group exercise at the end of session three will involve the seminar group coming to some closure as to how to deal with various screening difficulties. Parts of this class session could be videotaped and used in the fourth session. We use the "class video" before they show tapes of their own work. This way they can practice getting used to showing video. Trainees have a chance to first become comfortable with seeing each other on tape in a less vulnerable situation before exposing their therapy in front of their peers.

Sessions four, five, and six will address problems encountered in the first stage of time-limited group psychotherapy. A major issue in the beginning is how to establish realistic ground rules and a focus. Looking at the parallel between training and therapy, is there a major theme that the group members or the trainees have in common that brings them together? Are these similar developmental or training issues? Another focus for the seminar will involve the when and how of group versus individual interventions. How can a therapist most effectively enable patients to talk to one another, problem solve or acknowledge each other's contributions. Trainers will begin to discuss possible interventions with problematic group members at this point. Occasionally, a member may expose too much too early for the group to manage; for example, a patient might discuss a recent major loss of a family member through suicide.

Sessions seven, eight, and nine of the seminar will focus on the group crises. We expect that trainees might express dissatisfaction with the seminar just as members of a therapy group express disappointment in a group leader and the group in general. The challenge for the therapist or the trainer is how to be active in a manner that invites the group members to work with their feelings of disappointment in establishing realistic goals and expectations for the group. Part of creating useful training goals at this point is acknowledging that the group is half over and that time is limited.

Sessions ten, eleven, and twelve are usually the working meetings of the group as they will be the working meetings of the seminar. This is a time when the group is very focused on problem solving at a deeper level than previously experienced in the life of the group. We expect that trainees will become less reticent about evaluating each other's work at this stage. As the participants trust their colleagues more, they will feel freer to explore their work in depth.

The termination group sessions are number thirteen, fourteen and fifteen. This will be a time to address problems with closure, evaluation of objectives achieved, and saying good-bye. In some short-term groups, some members feel they have just begun while others who have been more focused and participatory have a sense of completion of an issue in their life. We expect that the seminar members will conduct a similar evaluation of accomplishments. They will also establish future goals for training.

CONCLUSION

The process of running short-term groups is intense and demanding. However, we have found that effective leadership can make a substantial difference in the outcome of the group. It is, therefore, important that therapists are well trained and feel confident and competent to do this work. The tasks of a short-term training program are twofold: first, the therapist must establish an awareness that short-term groups can be very useful and are not just poor substitutes for individual treatment or a long-term group. Secondly, the therapist must become an active facilitator of group process, who creates a forum for interpersonal learning within and outside the group. We propose that teaching the concepts discussed in this paper in a fifteen week training group provides clinicians a firsthand experience with some of the difficulties and triumphs involved in short-term group leadership.

REFERENCES

Budman, Simon H., and Gurman, Alan S. (1988). *The theory: Practice of brief therapy*, pp. 1-121; pp. 311-378. New York: Guilford Press.

Budman, Simon H. (1987). Preliminary findings on an instrument to measure cohesion in group psychotherapy. In *International Journal of Group Therapy*, pp. 75-94.

Daley, Barbara S., and Koppenaal, Geraldine (1981). The treatment of women in short-term women's groups. In S. H. Budman (Ed.), *Forms of brief therapy*. New York: Guilford Press.

Koppenaal, Geraldine and Ellis, Jane (1986). Emergency mental health care at an HMO. *Handbook of Emergency Psychology Clinical Administration*. Friedman, R. and Barton, G. New York: The Haworth Press, Inc.

Chapter 9

Teaching Gender Issues
to Male/Female Group Therapists

Karen Gail Lewis

INTRODUCTION

In the past few years, the number of articles about feminism,
feminism and social work, feminism and family therapy, feminism
and training, and feminism and psychoanalytic psychotherapy has
increased significantly. This is obviously a good time in the feminist field for so many diverse therapists are taking the issues seriously—looking at clinical theory and clinical practice. To the best
of my knowledge, little has been written on feminism and group
therapy, feminism in the co-leader relationship, and certainly not on
feminism and group therapy supervision. This article begins the
exploration of the overlap of these three factors: feminist issues in
supervision of group co-therapists.* Key feminist terms will be explained followed by a description of a gender sensitive group therapist, the co-therapy relationship, and the role of the supervisor in
attending to feminist issues in the supervision and in the group.

Karen Gail Lewis, ACSW, EdD, is Associate Professor at Catholic University
of America, National Catholic School of Social Services, Washington, DC.

---

*The terms co-leadership, co-therapists, and co-ed team will be used inter-
changeably, all referring to a joint male and female leadership of a therapy group.
It should be noted though, that the same issues need to be heeded when there is a
same sex co-leadership since the group may identify one leader as the male and
one as the female.

FEMINIST ISSUES IN THERAPY

Feminism is not a collection of techniques; it is a different lens for viewing relationships, life events, societal rules—in essence, reality. Feminism is

> a process that begins with the recognition of the inferior status of women, proceeds to an analysis of the specific forms and causes of that inequality, makes recommendations for strategies of change, and eventually leads to a recognition and validation of women's realities, women's interpretations, and women's contributions. (Wheeler, quoted in Wheeler, Avis, Miller, & Chaney, 1988, p. 53-54)

Gender is not to be confused with sex. Sex is a biological category; human beings are either males or females. Gender, however, is a social construct; society defines the tasks, behaviors, beliefs, and attitudes that become labeled masculine or feminine.

> Gender stereotyping results from regarding designated behaviors, attitudes, and feelings as appropriate to only one sex . . . [and we] act as if these are real, i.e., natural differences, rather than socially shaped; we forget that sex refers only to anatomical differences. (Goodrich, Rampage, Ellman, & Halstead, 1988, p. 5)

By looking at masculine and feminine traits, it is clear that society has defined the male gender as dominant and more valued, the female gender as subordinate and less valued. American society is proud of its individualism, autonomy, rationality, and power. Hierarchy is very important as demonstrated by the familiar phrase of "keeping up with (or surpassing) the Jones." The female traits of nurturance, affiliation, and interdependence have less societal value, and have been labeled by researchers as less mentally healthy (Broverman, Vogel, Clarkson, & Rosenkrantz, 1972).

Some of the key feminist issues include power, equality, and respect. While all three are important, without the first, the last two are not possible. Power is typically understood by its instrumental (masculine) meaning—having power over someone else; a hierarchical relationship where one is more powerful than another. Feminists, however, have defined power as

> control over choices and decisions concerning one's own life; control over the definition of one's relationships; the ability to influence others, especially one's mate; and access to resources and opportunities—economic, educational and vocational. (Avis, in press)

While women stereotypically have more influence or power within the home and in child rearing, men have more influence in most other areas including distribution of money, access to social power and recognition from the outside world.

Everyone needs a sense of personal power, yet recognition from the outside world is crucial for validation of that power. Typically men have that recognition as a contributing (working) member of society; women lack that validation by either not working or receiving less pay for the same job as a man. Men's physical power also needs to be recognized, for women may not feel equal in an argument if they know they may be physically abused. Further, if a man is unhappily married, he can divorce his wife, primarily losing companionship and housekeeping services. A woman, on the other hand, is less likely to leave a bad marriage since the stakes are higher and the losses are greater, e.g., the risk of losing custody, less income, less preparation for dealing with the working world, as well as companionship.

Because there is so much emotional overreaction to these ideas, it is important to be real clear: the issue is not simply who washes the dishes and who mows the lawn; the issue is how the decisions are made. Do women and men have an equal say about the division of labor or are the decisions automatically made based on gender stereotyping? Are the individual needs of the woman given as much consideration as the needs of the man? Reversing the stereotypical roles would not address this basic imbalance.

GENDER SENSITIVE GROUP THERAPISTS

Gender sensitive group therapists understand and emphasize the social context in which women and men live; they recognize the unique problems women face because of their familial and cultural socialization. They foster assertiveness and personal power in female clients; encourage women's flexibility in thinking about their vocational, sexual, familial, and personal choices. They recognize that what seem like personal inadequacies in women are often socially prescribed behaviors, not individual psychopathology. Gender sensitive therapists do not help women deal better with their ascribed roles; instead, they help them change the roles (Gurman & Klein, 1984). They support and validate women's work—both within and out of the home. Gender sensitive group therapists have an ethical responsibility to help clients see the power imbalance in their lives and to work towards the redistribution of power in their family (Jacobson, 1983) and in other aspects of their lives—including therapy.

Men, too, have been "victims of a sexist culture and its rigid patterns of socialization, [but] it is still men who hold the balance of power and receive a disproportionate share of social rewards and privileges" (Wheeler et al., 1988, p. 56). Gender sensitive group therapists recognize men's rigidified roles and help men work towards having more flexible choices. They help men acknowledge the power imbalance with women and make changes which will reap the benefits of a more equal relationship with women.

CO-THERAPY RELATIONSHIP

When a man and a woman co-lead a therapy group, their personal style and the style of their relationship color, to some extent, what happens in the therapy. In psychoanalytically oriented groups, the leaders are acutely aware of their relationship and its effect on the group in terms of parental transferences. Gender biases in their interpretation of the transference, though, are often overlooked. If a female group member responds to a male leader in a particular way, her behavior is understood (and interpreted) through a transferential lens. However, the reality base of her behavior—e.g., female learned behavior with males — is ignored. Co-therapists must consider the possibility that clients' behaviors and reactions may be a result of inhibiting gender stereotyping.

Co-therapists often are not co-equals. Often one is more experienced in therapy or in group therapy, or one sees him or herself as more senior than the other. Even if they are equal in terms of clinical experience, professional titles can be used to establish a hierarchy. Stereotypically, social workers are seen as being lower on the status ladder than psychologists and psychiatrists. Aside from these distinctions, one leader may be more comfortable in the group, or one talks more than the other, or one has a more dominant style. These differences have an influence on the group, especially on how it views the two leaders. One of the most common teams is the male psychologist/psychiatrist and the female social worker. Stereotypically, the male is taller, has a deeper voice, is called doctor, and comes across with more authority than the female who is shorter, has a softer voice, is called Ms., and speaks with less authority. All of this, of course, is irrelevant to the quality of their work, but not at all irrelevant to how they are perceived by the group members.

However, regardless of the leaders' personality styles and roles, the group as a whole and the individual group members may ascribe a specific gender based transferential role to each. The gender associations attached to the roles of the male and female leaders need to be addressed since the leaders are role models for the group members. If the leaders fit the stereotypical male/female roles, they are inadvertently telling their male clients that the male should be the leader and that the female should remain a good back-up. They are inadvertently telling the female clients that they are supposed to let the male take the lead.

While there are many possible combinations of styles between the leaders, two will be discussed here from the perspective of the female co-leader. The first is the female leader who is more senior, skilled, dominant, and comfortable with her leadership role (hereafter called dominant); the second is the more reserved female who lets the male co-therapist take the lead (hereafter called passive). Both of these styles will be exaggerated in order to accentuate the important aspects. The terms dominant and passive are not used pejoratively, rather as a reflection of how leaders in these two roles are typically perceived by group members.

Example One: Passive Female Co-Therapist

Warren, a psychologist in his early forties, and Clara, a social worker in her early thirties ran a co-ed therapy group. During one group session, Ellen verbally attacked the female leader. "I'm sick of it. You never talk. You just sit there; you don't do anything." Clara was stunned; before she could respond, several other women challenged Ellen, interpreting her need to attack a leader as a transference issue with her mother who had not been emotionally available to her when she was a young child. Warren reinforced this by speaking with pleasure that the group was able to make the connection between Ellen's behavior and her anger at her mother. This led to a direct discussion of Ellen's anger at her mother.

Example Two: Dominant Female Co-Therapist

One day in an all-women's group, Len and Gail, having equal skills and status as co-leaders, had a strong disagreement about an exercise Gail wanted to try. After a mutual discussion of the goal and instructions for the exercise, with Len offering some amendments, they agreed to go ahead. The exercise was productive.

The next day when one member mentioned the "fight," the leaders asked the group what they thought had happened. Lisa, who had previously described her mother as bitterly outspoken and her father as peripheral, said she was furious at Gail for dominating Len. Gail responded by saying, "You must see Len as pretty weak. . . . I wonder why you weren't angry at him for letting me dominate him." Len suggested Lisa may have been angry at him for letting Gail take charge, but by being angry at Gail instead was a way to protect him from her anger. This led to an avid discussion by the whole group of women's need to protect men.

What is the difference between these two examples? In the first, the attack on Clara was immediately followed by the group members intervening. Perhaps, they were protecting Clara or perhaps they were blocking their own feelings of anger at Clara's passivity. This was then followed by Warren's remark supporting the group's comment. In fact, Clara never did respond. While the transference issues probably were significant for Ellen, the real life situation with Clara only reinforced Ellen's experience that women are ineffectual. The parallel continued with Warren covering up for Clara just like Ellen's father had covered up for her mother (by saying nothing).

In the second example, the leaders saw the impact of their behavior and took the opportunity of their disagreement to help the members look at their association to male and female roles. The difference between this and the first example is not just that the leaders' response did not deal with parental transference — for that could just as easily have happened before or after the comments they did make. The major difference is that their comments openly addressed role stereotyping — as it was occurring in the group — which led to a more general discussion about how women carry their protective role into many situations.

Stereotypically and in my clinical experience, the female therapist is often quicker to pick up on the affect or to respond affectively than the male therapist who often is quicker to respond with suggestions of an "action." Even when this does not occur, clients may superimpose their traditional view onto the co-therapists. The gender sensitive group therapist listens for role-regulating behavior. As the two examples showed, female group members are more likely to protect the male therapist, overlooking sexist or domineering behavior and comments. They are more likely to accept the female leader's passivity since for so many that reflects their early role modeling. Therapists must help male and female group members not to automatically accept these behaviors but to hold them up for inspection. Some questions to help note gender issues in a therapy group include the following. Are the male clients the first to talk? If a male and female start to talk at the same time, does the female back down? Do the females give more support when the males are talking or are upset but say nothing when the males do not offer support when they are upset? Are the females subtly protective of the males, e.g., changing the topic when a male becomes teary, so the male does not have to address his own issues? When married women are talking about career or life choices, do they accept the traditional manner of decision making around child care, household chores, financial expenditure, money, parenting, or do they consider flexible options for each of these topics?

ROLE OF THE SUPERVISOR

The supervisor's role is extremely complex. There are at least five levels of activity that occur in all supervisory sessions, and the supervisor must attend to each: the supervisor and the supervisees, the supervisees themselves, the supervisees/therapists and the group, the group as a whole, and the individual group members. This is obviously an incomplete list since each level can be broken into several smaller parts. Further, each level has both a content and process agenda. The meaning of what occurs at each level must be understood for its concrete or digital messages and for its metaphorical or analogic messages (Haley, 1976). One of the things that makes the cacophony manageable is the repetitive patterns. Much has been written about the isomorphism (Liddle & Saba, 1982; 1983) or the parallel process (Yalom, 1975) that exists between the supervision and the therapy group.

> The supervisory session is no less a microcosm than the therapy group, and the supervisor should be able to obtain much information about the therapist's behavior in his therapy group by attending to his behavior in supervision. (Yalom, 1975, p. 507)

Behavior patterns, styles, and sometimes specific issues that occur within the group are repeated in the supervisory session. Areas where the group members or the co-therapists have difficulty are often the same areas that isomorphically cause difficulty in the supervision — either directly or covertly. For example, in a group struggling with dependency issues, the leaders may become uncharacteristically dependent in their supervision.

As the leaders report on what happened in the group the supervisor gains a sense of the issues that are conflictual across all five levels. Since gender issues are often not openly mentioned, it is through the parallel process occurring in the supervision that the supervisor can learn about gender-critical issues in the group. The group therapy supervisor has a responsibility to raise questions about the co-therapy relationship and its effect on the group.

> The clinical supervisor has a most immediate potential as mentor and positive role model. Gender as it affects both the supervision and the therapy process should be an explicit dimension of the supervisory contract, regardless of the gender makeup of the supervisory dyad. (Libow, 1986, p. 20)

Actually, group supervision is the most likely place to look at the effect of gender myths and rigidified roles since groups are a laboratory for dealing with problematic issues in everyday life. As a first step the supervisor must help the co-therapists look at their own gender issues; then at the group's reaction to them and the inherent gender issues in their transference to the leaders; and finally, at the gender issues that are relevant in the group members' lives.

Co-Therapists' Gender Issues

Since there is such suspicion and distortions about the concept of gender, the supervisor must help co-leaders understand that feminism does not blame men nor does it intend to divide the sexes. A feminist or non-sexist approach to therapy starts with the belief that ". . . none of us is personally responsible for the world we have inherited, but only for what we do with it" (Avis, in press).

In order to appreciate the breadth of gender biases — those culturally instilled and those handed down through the family of origin — male and female group therapists need to understand their own biases. They need to identify sexist attitudes and behaviors within their own lives and to understand the role their own gender has played in their handling of money, power, competence, and fairness. They need to recognize the effect these issues have had on the person they have become and on how they act. As they begin to understand these issues within their own lives and how they get played out between them in their roles as male and female and as co-therapists, they will have a clearer sense of how they interfere within the group and in individual group members' lives.

Male-female power differences between the co-therapists will almost assuredly occur. When it does happen within the supervision, it needs to be addressed. The supervisor may note that the male therapist always starts talking in the supervisory session. She can then ask which co-therapist talks first in the group. The type of questions she can ask include the following: Are confrontations to group members usually initiated by the male co-leader? Is the female co-leader the one who usually initiates an empathic response to grief or sadness?

It has been found that males talk more often in the supervision and interrupt the females who tend to be more hesitant in expressing their ideas (Avis, in press; Libow, 1986; Wheeler et al., 1988). When this occurs, the supervisor can model feminist concepts by dealing with this in a non-blaming, non-judgmental, yet gently confrontive manner. The point is to demonstrate the reality of what has just occurred. If group therapists become aware of how they automatically assume gender specific roles, it will be easier for them to see it in the group and to hear it as group members talk about their everyday lives. Change is obviously difficult, so the co-therapists may have to make a (self) conscious effort to assure a distribution and flexibility of roles between them.

Related to the power issue is hierarchy. Supervisors must work towards equalizing their relationship with supervisees. While the supervisees need to have "maximum participation and control over their own learning" (Avis, in press), this does not mean the supervisor abdicates responsibility for providing structure and guidance. Clearly she knows more about gender issues and group therapy, but she does not know it all. A non-hierarchical supervision leaves room for the supervisees to participate in their own creative learning process.

This equality of responsibility (not of knowledge) can be crystallized by a contract between the supervisor and the supervisee that establishes mutual responsibility for learning: understanding the problems, designing interpretations, creating interventions, and offering solutions (Wheeler et al., 1988). The contract should include opportunity for mutual evaluations — for supervisees and for supervisor. It should include a statement supporting the use of non-sexist language and examination of sexist behaviors or comments during the supervision. The underlying significance of such a contract is to highlight the non-hierarchical relationship that exists in the supervision. This same equality can then be carried over into the therapy group with the therapists having a contract with each group member outlining the goals of treatment and the responsibility of both the therapist and the client.

Obviously, to be able to help the co-therapists with these issues, the supervisor needs to listen carefully for gender biases within herself, in the supervision, and in the therapy group. This does not mean that the supervisor should expect to be totally free from gender biases and distortions, nor to expect supervisees ever to be. However, it does mean the supervisor needs to model the issues she is teaching the co-leaders. While she clearly is more experienced in group therapy than the co-therapists, she does not need to assume the expert role. She needs to share her own humanness, vulnerability, and mistakes. It is most useful for her to share her ongoing process of learning about gender issues — not to present herself as a "completed" gender-conscious person.

Gender Issues in the Group

The supervisor must help the co-therapists look for gender related issues within the group. While there are multiple issues that may occur in the group, three particular topics will be mentioned: reinforcement of traditional roles, women blaming, and father idealizing.

The leaders need to be aware how much of the group members' response to them is framed by traditional gender roles. They can start by noticing if there is a difference in how the whole group or individual members respond to each leader. What roles do group members automatically expect each leader to fulfill? For example, do they look to the male therapist for advice and to the female for sympathy? Is more credence put on the comments from one therapist than the other? Is one therapist ignored or discounted? In addition to what the supervisor may do based on a theoretical orientation, the leaders must be reminded that people have been raised to respond differently to males and females and especially males and females in authority positions. To give pathological interpretations to these culturally induced behaviors or comments does an injustice to the client. More relevant is to help clients see the rigidified roles and understand how these roles have inhibited their growth and limited their development.

As in the example of Len and Gail, the supervisor might suggest the co-therapists use incidences where gender stereotyping occurs as an opportunity to raise the question of how group members have learned to have different expectations of men and of women. What myths and roles have been passed down to them in their families that they have accepted without questioning, such as women should show sensitivity and interest (often by asking men questions), and men should show their competence or initiative? When these complementary roles occur in the group, the leaders can interrupt to point it out. The therapists can ask the women if they recognize their accommodating role; do they feel any anger about it; do they rationalize it away, or do they blame themselves for being so critical? The therapist can ask men if they recognize when they interrupt women who are talking or when they discount (or devalue) an idea because it comes from a women.

Another theme that needs vigilant attention is women blaming (Avis & Haig, 1988). This consists of placing responsibility for change more with the women than with the men. A common example occurs when female group members are asked why they allow men to monopolize the group. Much of the group therapy literature suggests this tactic as an appropriate comment when any one member dominates the group (Yalom, 1975). However, when women are blamed for not confronting males, the message becomes too similar to the covert message they have heard all their lives: they are responsible for the well-being (or the affective development) of males. Other common examples of women blaming occur when the therapist blames a woman for staying in a bad marriage, for not speaking up to an abusive husband or male friend, for not noticing a husband's incestuous behavior with a daughter, for not challenging a dominant boss, for not taking a firmer hand in dealing with an out of control child while the husband remains distant from the problem. The list is endless.

The third topic is closely related to mother blaming—father idealization. While most competent group therapists would notice when a client is idealizing a father, it is noticed but not addressed. When clients focus on the errors of their mother, the father's behavior escapes notice. The expectation is that mothers should be loving, available, etc.; fathers' non-involvement is accepted as normal or typical. Mothers then receive the blame while fathers are excused. Therapists should ask potent questions, such as why father did not notice or do anything when mother was being verbally or physically abusive. A typical response is that he was not home much or he did not see it. That is the reality of the situation, but it is not a satisfactory explanation. Therapists need to reiterate that a child deserves to be protected and cared for; when there are two parents, both must be held responsible for what happens to the child. Therapists owe it to their clients to help them recognize the neglect of both parents, rather than just assume mother should have been a better parent.

Gender Issues in the Lives of Individual Group Members

In my teaching and supervising, I often ask how many women were raised with the overt or covert message that a woman may be smarter than her brothers but she is not to let them know. Not surprisingly, most women recognize the dictum. The surprise, though, is for the men in the room who are usually oblivious to this message. Most women have unquestionably accepted the rule—perhaps unconsciously—and have geared their lives so that they are not more successful than their brothers or than men in general. They may be working against their innate abilities and establishing road blocks to self-fulfillment. Often they develop a symptom which gives them an excuse for not being successful (Lewis, 1987, 1988); this allows them to remain true to their family code. Women need to be challenged about the solutions they automatically assume are closed off to them or that they have discounted because of their gender or of family myths.

Men, at least in my unofficial sample, are unaware of these female rules; they do not know they are playing by different standards. This may account for their anger when accused of chauvinism. They need to learn the unspoken rules that woman have been obeying, for these rules harm men as well as women.

In group therapy, the men and women need to be challenged about the covert roles that are automatically assigned to them. These rules govern the inequality between them and effect so much of their lives: their relationship with others, their career choices, and their level of competence. Group members need to understand all of the covert rules. While the focus of the group may not be gender awareness, it behooves the leaders to help individual members see the effect of these rules on who they have become and on their life choices. The group, already a laboratory for examining relationships, provides a safe forum for looking at the debilitating effects of these gender prescribed rules.

CONCLUSION

Group therapy is a most logical place for people to be talking about what inhibits them from a fuller life. Regardless of the supervisors' theoretical orientation about symptom causation, traditional gender roles hinder women's fuller development and interfere with males reaching their full potential in intimacy and relationships. Without an appreciation for both the affiliative *and* the instrumental dimensions of their personality, both men and women lose.

If in supervision the therapists have a chance to see their own patterns of dealing with gender, they will be more acutely sensitive to spotting and gently confronting sexist comments or beliefs among the group members. For her part, the supervisor needs to beware of recreating the same problems that occur for men and women in society or in the group, that is, treating the woman as victim and making the man defensive. If both sexes feel empowered within the supervision, they are more likely to bring that acceptance and empowerment back into the group. The supervisor needs to help the male and female co-therapists integrate their expressive and instrumental (rational/cognitive) dimensions—both within the supervision and within the group.

REFERENCES

Avis, J. (In press). Integrating gender into the family therapy curriculum. *Journal of Feminist Family Therapy*.

Avis, J., & Haig, C. (1988). Woman-blaming in major family therapy journals. Paper presented to the 46th Annual Meeting of the American Association for Marriage and Family Therapy. New Orleans.

Broverman, I., Vogel, S.R., Broverman, D.M., Clarkson, F.E., & Rosenkrantz, P.S. (1972). Sex role stereotypes: A current appraisal. *Journal of Social Issues*, *28*, 59-78.

Goodrich, T.J., Rampage, C., Ellman, B., & Halstead, K. (1988). *Feminist family therapy*. New York: Norton

Gurman, A., & Klein, M. (1980). Marital and family conflicts. In A. Brodsky & R. Hare-Mustin (Eds.), *Women and psychotherapy*. New York: Guilford Press.

Haley, J. (1976). *Problem-solving therapy*. San Francisco: Jossey-Bass.

Jacobson, N. (1983). Beyond empiricism: The politics of marital therapy. *American Journal of Family Therapy*, *11*, 11-24.

Lewis, K.G. (1987). Bulimia as a communication to siblings. *Psychotherapy*, *24*, 640-645.

Lewis, K.G. (1988). Symptoms as sibling messages. In M. Kahn & K.G. Lewis (Eds.), *Siblings in therapy: Life span and clinical issues*. New York: Norton.

Libow, J. (1986). Training family therapists as feminists. In M. Ault-Riche (Ed.), *Women and family therapy*. Rockville, MD: Aspen Systems.

Liddle, H., & Saba, G. (1982). On teaching family therapy at the introductory level: A conceptual model emphasizing a pattern which connects training and therapy. *Journal of Marital and Family Therapy*, *8*, 63-72.

Liddle, H., & Saba, G. (1983). In context replication: The isomorphic nature of training and therapy. *Journal of Strategic and Systemic Therapies*, *2*, 3-11.

Wheeler, D., Avis, J., Miller, L, & Chaney, S. (1986). Rethinking family therapy education and supervision: A feminist model. In F. Piercy (Ed.), *Family therapy education and supervision*. New York: Haworth Press.

Yalom, I. (1975). Second Edition. *The theory and practice of group psychotherapy*. New York: Basic Books.

ON THE BOOKS

Karen Gail Lewis, Book Review Editor

NOTE. The books reviewed here are all related to groups. The first one is on children's group therapy. The next two address important issues of time and highlight the need for a more comprehensive theory of change that emphasizes the awareness of time and the use of this awareness in more effective ways.

Mary San Martino, LICSW
Boston, MA

CHILD GROUP PSYCHOTHERAPY: FUTURE TENSE. Riester, Albert E. and Kraft, Irvin A. (Eds.). *Madison, Connecticut: International Universities Press, Inc., 1986, 289 pp., $30.*

This book makes its appearance at a time when new inpatient and outpatient mental health programs for children are being established in every region of our country. The shortage of clinicians knowledgeable and trained in psychotherapy with children is acute. The value of the healing power of child group psychotherapy is accepted by many clinicians who often form these groups without sufficient training and experience. Thus, this book offers rich, valuable content and direction for clinicians and as Saul Scheidlinger states in the forward, it is long overdue. Scheidlinger comments that although child group psychotherapy has been practiced since 1930, this is the first book to include all of the essential elements that need to be taught in a course on child group psychotherapy.

The book is organized into six sections and provides an historic perspective from the initial writings of S.R. Slavson to the contributions of present day clinicians. Each section has a specific focus including the following topics: a developmental perspective in planning childrens groups; the place of diagnostic play groups; groups for special populations and problems, and in special settings; issues for the child group psychotherapist, such as countertransference, and the importance of supervised experience in training; and the critical need for reliable and valid research about child group psychotherapy. The chapters of the book are contributed by 14 child group psychotherapists who have been the leaders and standard setters for this treatment modality.

The first chapter by the coeditors Albert Riester and Irvin Kraft describes the changes, adaptations, and modifications that have occurred in the historical evolution of child group psychotherapy. While practical problems of space, time and a large pool of group prospects have caused a decrease in the use of the original model of Activity Group Therapy (AGT) developed by Slavson, other modifications such as Activity-Interview Group Therapy (AIGT) have emerged. Riester and Kraft describe six different methods centering on verbalizations in group interaction and strongly recommend that clinicians continue to form groups for appropriate children even in private practice settings with a small pool of prospects, and even if the group must begin with just two children. Slavson's chapter, originally published in 1945, that described the healing power of groups and how experiences in eight basic groups in society contribute to personality development leads up to current child group practice described by Gerald Schamess. Schamess has integrated the essentials of group structure such as space, time, play materials, and activity of therapist with recent refinements of theories of personality development. Schamess achieves this goal by linking group selection and planning to the child's phase-specific developmental needs as well as DSM-III diagnosis and level of character pathology. Schamess includes a literature review to demonstrate how different models of group methodology have been initiated according to level of pathology, such as developmental deviations, borderline conditions, psychosis and neurotic organization. Schamess' chapter is an extremely valuable contribution as it blends together levels of development and psychopathology with group dynamics, and captures the complexity of child group psychotherapy. As Schamess cautions, clinicians who attempt to form children's groups without carefully considering these three interdependent areas of theory often experience failure and withdraw from the practice of child group psychotherapy in frustration and discouragement.

Jerome Liebowitz and Paulina Kernberg describe the value of observing a child in peer group play during the diagnostic evaluation. They say that the diagnostic play group is not commonly used in child mental health settings, but that other aspects of the child's personality structure not seen in the individual evaluation will emerge in the group. Beryce MacLennan reviews the various settings in which child group psychotherapy is practiced, such as inpatient and outpatient settings, schools, and in crisis situations. Thomas Gaines discusses specific applications of child group psychotherapy such as parallel group therapy for parents, social skills groups, groups for children of divorce, and groups for abused children. The chapter by Judy Crawford-Brobyn and Andrea White focuses on a model they developed for treatment of impulse-ridden latency age children. The model was developed in response to the increase in impulse-ridden, aggressive, and destructive boys referred for treatment. Quite often these children are rightly viewed as lacking social skills and having poor peer relations and needing to develop peer relationship skills. They are often referred for group psychotherapy but are so demanding and disruptive that they are not appropriate for many latency groups. If added to a group without careful screening and planning, it may lead to the child having to be removed and result in another rejection for the child. Crawford-Brobyn and White base their model on social learning theory as it relates to social skills acquisition and describe a process of progression from a dyad of two boys paired for similar styles and characteristics to later movement into a group.

The next three chapters deal with demands and personal characteristics of the therapist in child group psychotherapy. Fern Azima discusses the important area of countertransference, particularly as it is triggered off by the regressive and primitive behavior of children, and magnified further if such behavior becomes contagious in the group and leads to chaos. Azima points out that countertransference reactions not only arise within the therapist and the psychotherapy process but from interaction with the children, the group, treatment team, parents and others in the surrounding community network. Azima describes such countertransference reactions as intellectualization, boredom, smothering, overidentification with child or parent, and offers suggestions for reducing countertransference. Azima's discussion leads naturally to Edward Soo's chapter on the training and supervision of child group psychotherapists. Soo lists the following three components of training: (1) individual supervision which addresses the supervisee's specific learning needs, knowledge of children's group psychotherapy, and the understanding of clinical material; (2) the training group which allows the trainee to experience the emotional impact of group formation and dynamics, understand subgroup and group resistances, and observe the supervisor's activity in the group; and (3) the supervisory group in which supervisees must experience peer support and trust before they can risk presenting their work with groups of children for discussion. Soo also agrees that childrens' groups reawaken infantile conflicts in the therapists and that the supervisory group is useful for identifying objective countertransference reactions that emerge from the patient group members and process.

The next chapter in the book is written by Robert Dies and Albert Riester and is a comprehensive review of Research on Child Group Therapy. The literature review resulted in 18 anecdotal reports and 22 research reports. Dies and Riester are quite critical of the quality of the reports and the minimal application of research methodology for learning about the process and benefits of child group psychotherapy. They delineate three steps for improving the level of sophistication beyond the vast majority of the reports they reviewed.

The final section of the book includes two chapters that point to the future of child group psychotherapy. Mortimer Schiffer reviews the basic methodology and features of Activity Group Therapy (AGT) and is critical of modifications of AGT over the years. His criticism is based on the view that many clinicians do not understand the value and benefits of AGT and modify the method because of inexperience, insufficient training, and lack of supervision. Schiffer does acknowledge that because of the growing numbers of ego-impaired, impulse-ridden children that modifications of AGT have had to be made. Schiffer cautions that efforts to modify AGT should be studied and evaluated carefully in order not to lose the unique curative strengths of AGT.

The final chapter by Irvin Kraft addresses innovative and creative approaches in child group psychotherapy, such as the use of audiovisual aids like tape recorders and VCRs. The use of object-centered techniques to produce expressive play include anatomically correct dolls, bean bag chairs, video games, athletics, and carefully planned field trips. The ability to flexibly modify the process of the group because of life events and crises of group members can offer therapeutic benefits if planned carefully.

This is an excellent book that deals in depth with the essential theoretical and methodological features of child group psychotherapy. This reviewer agrees with Saul Scheidlinger that the organization and content of this book make it an essential basic text in any course or training seminar in child group psychotherapy, as well as a valuable addition to the libraries of experienced child group psychotherapists.

James F. Kennedy, PhD
Assistant Professor
Director of Group Psychotherapy
for Children and Adolescents
Child Psychiatric Services
University of Louisville School of Medicine
Louisville, KY

TIME AS A FACTOR IN GROUP WORK: TIME-LIMITED
GROUP EXPERIENCES. Allissi, A. S. and Casper, M. (Eds.).
New York: The Haworth Press, Inc., 1985, 160 pp., $19.95.

This special issue of *Social Work with Groups* devotes itself to
the issue of time as a significant variable in a variety of group work
situations. In as much as time has become a scarce and expensive
commodity as well as the center of every person's awareness, the
editors emphasize that there can no longer be a timeless practice. A
selection of papers are presented to discuss time in terms of effectiveness of service and sensivity to the human condition.

Three major premises predominate. First, time limits can be used
positively. Second, the emphasis on present, ongoing processess in
group interaction is a noticeable shift from past practice. Third, it
becomes the mission of the group leader to make the best use of
limited time with a level of "high intensity" activity. These premises have an existential quality.

The contributions in this valuable little book focus on specific
goals which provide structure and boundaries for the time-limited
experience. These goals are often the same as less limited time
frames. The difference is in the specificity of content and in the
increased and heightened use of activity and purpose which is mod-
eled and encouraged by the leader.

A variety of settings and age groups with specific tasks are presented. Time-limited group work with children is discussed by
Steven R. Rose as part of a comprehensive effort of social agencies
to adopt a brief intervention model. Persuasive evidence is given to
illustrate the effectiveness of this model to promote better social
functioning in children with a variety of problems.

The life cycle model is apparent in the paper by Lisa R. Block,
"On Potentiality and Limits of Time: The Single Session Group
and the Cancer Patient." The single session group with CA patients
presents a challenge to the leader to make the greatest use of time in
a group in which individual members have an acute awareness of
their own deaths. Although widely used in hospital settings, little
has been written as to the specific demands on the leader in planning and running such a group effectively.

Open-ended groups make specific demands on leaders. M. J. Galinsky and J. Schopler offer a good beginning discussion of the skills required to run such groups in "Patterns of Entry and Exit in Open-Ended Groups."

These are a few of the valuable contributions in this collection. The rest are all pertinent and interesting. This volume represents a needed beginning look at time-limited group work in various settings with different tasks.

Similar efforts in the fields of time-limited psychotherapy as well as family therapy reflect some of the same premises present in this collection and highlight the need for a more comprehensive theory of change that emphasizes the awareness of time and the use of this awareness in more effective ways.

Mary San Martino, LICSW
Boston, MA

RESEARCH IN SOCIAL GROUP WORK. Feldman, Ronald Q., and Rose, Sheldon D. (Eds.). *New York: The Haworth Press, Inc., 1986, 124 pp., $34.95.*

The book, *Research in Social Group Work* is essentially a hardbound edition of the journal *Social Work with Groups* (Vol. 9, No. 3, 1986). The book consists of a guest editorial (by Feldman), followed by seven articles on some aspect of group work research.

As a journal issue, this set of articles is bound by a slender, but common thread in that all the articles address some aspect of social group work research. As a book, however, this volume seems plagued by an inability to establish its purpose, to define its place in the pantheon of books on this topic. It is neither a book about salient methodological issues in groupwork research, nor is it a "how-to" book on the evaluation of clinical treatment in groups, although both types of articles are represented.

The book begins with Feldman's guest editorial, a review and classification of all group work articles contained in seven selected journals, from 1975 (their inception) to 1983. These figures are then compared to those from an earlier review (1966) in order to discern trends in the expansion of this knowledge base. Other than a notable increase in the publication of research-based articles, the review reveals relatively little interest.

Glisson's article on the implications of selection of the individual versus the group as the unit of analysis is excellent: it provides a clear explanation of the problem, followed by an example which illustrates the phenomena the author seeks to illuminate. The article by Tallent on meta-analyses similarly focuses on a broad methodological issue with considerable success.

The Garvin article on task-centered group work with chronic mental patients, and the Subramanian article on group treatment for pain management focus on intervention with well-defined client groups. Garvin's article applies a developmental research framework to the problem, taking the reader step-by-step through the planning, recruitment, intervention design, and evaluation phase. The article is clearly written, and the tasks well articulated: this may well be the best article in the volume. The Subramarian article, on the other hand, is a rather curious addition. In three rather short paragraphs, the author runs through the treatment format, the methods used, and the results. The latter paragraph mentions "statistically significant differences between experimental and control groups," but not a single test of significance is ever mentioned. In fact, the author devotes considerable space to anecdotal material, an oddity in a "research-based" article.

The three remaining articles in the book represent a mix in terms of their focus. The article by Goldberg and Lamont, one of three in the book written expressly for this issue, represents the greatest departure in subject matter. These authors studied the impact of curriculum shift (from one in which the curriculum was organized around 5 different practice strands, to a generic focus) upon the acquisition of a sound knowledge base and practice competence in group work. Measuring students' self-perceived competence and knowledge in this area both before and after the curriculum change, they found that the curriculum model to which students are exposed does impact upon these two variables, and that the generic model is inferior in this regard. The fact that these results fly in the face of the conventional wisdom about curriculum development makes this article interesting. Furthermore, their bibliography reveals a paucity of research. However, as these authors point out, their measures of knowledge (a 14 item "quiz" requiring the student to match book titles with authors) and competence (self-perceived) are of questionable validity; thus, further exploration in this area is warranted.

Joseph Anderson offers an alternative model of combining research and practice to the developmental model discussed by Garvin. Briefly, this author calls for the application of single system instrumentation to evaluate group process as well as the outcome in terms of student group member improvement. Although interesting, the author brings little new to the knowledge construction enterprise in this field. In fact, the major points in his paper (on instrumentation and single-system design) rely heavily on the work of one author and seem not to go sufficiently beyond the work of this individual to be considered new knowledge.

Finally, Rose et al. report on the interim research results and process used in a research development program of a "multimethod group approach to the treatment of a wide variety of stress related presenting problems." The broad contours of the approach are mapped out. With its emphasis on individualization, environmental modification, and the maintenance of individual dignity, the model is most consistent with social work values.

The authors apply their model to three broad problems: chronic stress, pain management, and spousal abuse. In each case, the authors vigorously apply their model, test their results, and modify when necessary. In many ways, the approach is similar to Garvin's and, as Garvin did, these authors provide us with a clearly written piece about an exemplary treatment/research model.

This book is recommended only for those who, of course, do not subscribe to the journal from which this issue came but who aspire to build extensive libraries in this field. The uneven quality of the articles within, and the amorphous nature of the book prevent its recommendation as a text.

Alice A. Lieberman, PhD
University of Kansas School of Social Welfare
Lawrence, KS

GAME PLAY THERAPEUTIC GAMES FOR CHILDREN. Schaefer, Charles E. and Reid, Steven E. (Eds.). *New York: John Wiley & Sons, 1986, 349 pp.*

As a playful therapist, myself, I was delighted to review *Game Play*. This edited volume recognizes game playing as an integral part of the socialization of children, and offers a variety of ways in which games can have a significant role in the therapeutic process. It also suggests types of games, games for particular populations, and how games can be used for diagnostic and treatment purposes.

The book is divided into four parts. Chapters in the first section deal with games of communication. These are designed to encourage self-expression and self-disclosure on the part of children who are reluctant or resistant or those who may have specific problems in communicating. Through games, a patient has a chance to express feelings, conflicts, and issues that may otherwise remain covert and/or displaced. Through the game playing, patients can become more open in their relationship with the therapist and in the therapeutic process itself.

The second section of the book involves problem solving games. These are generally more structured and primarily involve cognitive functioning. They are designed to help a child figure out specific problem areas, such as those arising in divorce or remarriage situations. Games in this category also foster general problem solving skills.

The third section focuses on ego-enhancing games. Competitive in nature, they deal with rules and strategies for winning. Issues that arise here include the need to win, cheating, feelings of competence, self-worth, disappointment, aggression, etc. In addition, chapters suggest ways such games may help develop skills in children with specific deficits such as impulsivity, fine-motor incoordination or learning disabilities.

The last section of the book uses games to modify social behavior. Done in group situations, the activities range from specific behaviors to be positively reinforced in the group to activities that address more complex real life social situations. Their efficacy in work with special groups, like the mentally retarded or delinquents, is illustrated.

Game Play provides a broad spectrum of games, both well-known and those more newly created, many by the authors. Although the chapters provide lots of rich detail and clinical examples of how the games can be used in specific therapeutic situations, with particular clinical populations, the volume's scope is much broader.

The authors emphasize the therapeutic use of games as being part of a larger treatment context, not as an end in itself. The special value in play is in its creation of an atmosphere that is familiar and pleasurable to children. Its diagnostic use does not appear invasive or threatening. It is a way to join with youngsters who may otherwise have difficulty engaging in therapy. In this regard, the importance of the child's developing relationship with the therapist, with important others (family, friends) is sensitively acknowledged. This modality, applied with openness and enthusiasm to children whom many would consider untreatable, offers a positive, hopeful, even fun side for working with some very difficult populations.

The book also does what it talks about. The content and style of the chapters invite the reader to a warm and pleasurable experience. Once involved, I found myself becoming more open in thinking about ways I could broaden my perspective on therapy, and on my relationships with my patients. The volume gave me ideas on how I could expand my therapy skills. It also gave me permission to create my own new ways of working..

Not a cook book, *Game Play* is a resource for the ever developing therapist.

Ann Itzkowitz, MA
Director, Adolescent Unit
Child and Family Inpatient Service
Philadelphia Child Guidance Clinic
Philadelphia, PA